Great Saints,
Great Friends

Great Saints,
Great Friends

Mary Neill, OP *and* Ronda Chervin

ALBA · HOUSE   NEW · YORK

SOCIETY OF ST. PAUL, 2187 VICTORY BLVD., STATEN ISLAND, NEW YORK 10314

Library of Congress Cataloging-in-Publication Data

Neill, Mary.
      Great saints, great friends / Mary Neill and Ronda Chervin.
          p.   cm.
      ISBN 0-8189-0574-3
      1. Christian saints — Biography.   I. Chervin, Ronda.   II. Title.
      BX4657.N45   1989
      282'.092'2 — dc20   89-28931
      [B]   CIP

Designed, printed and bound in the United States of
America by the Fathers and Brothers of the
Society of St. Paul, 2187 Victory Boulevard,
Staten Island, New York 10314, as part of their
communications apostolate.

Printing Information:

Current Printing - first digit   2 3 4 5 6 7 8 9 10 11 12

Year of Current Printing - first year shown
  1990   1991   1992   1993   1994   1995   1996   1997

Preface I

Mary Neill

Sacrifice, writes the poet Rainer Maria Rilke, is ". . . the boundless resolve, no longer limitable in any direction, to achieve one's purest possibility." (Letter of February, 1914) Elsewhere, he says of pain:

> How we squander our hours of pain.
> How we gaze beyond them into the bitter
> duration to see if they have an end. Though they
> are really our winter-enduring foliage,
> our dark ever green, one season in our inner
> year — not only a season in time —,
> but are place and settlement,
> foundation and soil and home.

> ("The Tenth Elegy" from *The Selected Poetry of Rainer Maria Rilke*, tr. by Stephen Mitchell ([NY: Vintage Books, 1984], p. 205).

These two quotations illuminate for me what seems the central struggle of my own life: where do I find the source of energy, the direction to find my "purest possibility" — my deepest heart's desire — my calling that is mine and no other's?

What must I sacrifice to find this source of energy? What are the secondary possibilities that are the ultimate temptation — fine things themselves, but distraction from my deepest directions?

Furthermore, how am I to honor the pain involved in such a search for source and calling? How am I not to squander my pain; how to find it not punishment but purification? How am I to believe that the wounding of such a process is God making place for Himself so that I may come to find Him, and my truest self deep within, as "place and settlement, foundation and soil and home"?

I, who find myself so often "soul-less and displaced" and unconnected, seek connection with those whose lives declare that they are not orphans. They belong to someone: to themselves, to others, to God. Having been rescued from homelessness, they are a home to others.

Sometimes these "homemakers" are living men and women. Sometimes I find these persons in books so strongly vibrant with love and life that they leap from the pages to encourage me to live the Good News. There are the saints, my companions on the way, friends against despair, calling me to become more alive to God, and dead to faithlessness.

Several years ago when I visited the leper colony at Molakai, I experienced how deeply I had been moved as a teenager by the story of Father Damien, who had brought faith and love and hope and clothes and medicine and brotherhood to lepers abandoned by society to their pain and affliction. Fiercely, even impatiently and fanatically, he had made a clearing in the forest of their pain and said, "I care: I am a sign of God's love to you. I am not afraid of touching you, or becoming one of you."

As I stood in the abandoned church where he had announced to them his ultimate bonding by beginning his sermon,

"*We* lepers . . ." I felt awed by such love. I felt him there. I felt the same God he loved calling me to believe that I, too, was made by Love for love.

Father Damien, a real person, like me had stood there, love pouring out from his body to heal the homeless. His life gives meaning to my search, to find my purest possibility, as he had found his.

So often the search seems unreal; the calling, an insanity — not really normal, you know. But when my feet stood on the same boards where Father Damien's feet had stood, and my eyes saw the same bay that lepers had been tossed into to swim as best they could from ship to shore, my body as well as my mind knew that the search for God's love was the only thing that mattered. For that moment, I was touching home; I knew I was in the right direction.

I remember being appalled to read that Teresa of Avila's dead body was parcelled into relic fragments within a day or two of her death, so anxious were those who loved her to have a piece of her. I understand that impulse better now — the need to touch that body so obviously touched by God. Saints seem to me like great lamps of light and love, burning up their bodies to feed that light. Thick and muddied, our bodies often flicker but faintly with world-encompassing love energies. So we long to touch such a holy body, even long dead, or a piece of cloth that touched that body — or a cloth that touched the tomb that held that body. I have such a relic of St. Dominic.

Incarnationalists all, we respond to the embodiment of love. Holy men and women, like Christ, are God's love turning to touch us. We find ourselves thinking of them, as of Christ.

As Huston Smith writes: ". . . if God is pure goodness, if he were to take human form this is the way he would act." (*The Religions of Man* ([NY: Harper and Row, 1974], p. 304)

Captive to fear and ignorance and distractions, we long to

be free in the way saints are free. Again, Huston Smith's description of sanctity enlightens us:

"They seem free, not in the sense that they go around breaking the laws of nature (though the power to do exceptional things, which could seem like miracles to us, is usually ascribed to them) but in the sense that they never find the natural order frustrating. This being so, nothing binds them nor shakes them . . . nothing disrupts their peace of mind. They feel no lack, no misery, no fear, and find no cause for strife or grief. They seem always to be in good spirits, agreeable, even gay. As their egos need no bolstering, their love can flow outward alike to all. Contact with them imparts strength, purity and encouragement." (Smith, p. 32)

I'm not sure that I agree that saints don't feel lack or misery or fear. I understand them as feeling and experiencing these negative forces, but not *defining* themselves by these states. Their soul and foundation is eternal in God and this has become their central identity. God is the ocean within, on whose surface storms may play, but the depths are at peace.

An indissoluble marriage of opposites had taken place — divinity and humanity within. The energy and fruits of that union are so apparent in the life and work of the saints that nothing can shake that marriage. As Paul so piercingly writes:

"Who will separate us from the love of Christ? Trial or distress or persecution or hunger or nakedness or danger or the sword? As Scripture says: for your sake we are being slain all the day long; we are looked upon as sheep to be slaughtered. Yet in all this we are more than conquerors because of Him who loved us. For I am certain that neither death nor life, neither angels nor principalities, neither the present nor the future, nor powers, neither height nor depth or any other creature, will be able to separate us from the love of God that comes to us in Christ Jesus, our Lord." (Romans 8:35-39)

Christ, the purest possibility of humankind; Christ who never squandered His pain, even calling "Abba, Abba," as the darkness descended before which He knelt, the Prince of Peace and of Pain — He is the Alpha and Omega of Christian godliness, the saint-maker par excellence, the clarion call to find God incarnate in our bodies, in all bodies the seal and sign that God loves us in personal and passionate and tenderest individuality.

Preface II

Ronda Chervin

"There is only one tragedy, not to have been a saint," wrote Leon Bloy. Ever since becoming a Catholic some twenty-five years ago, the lives of the saints have fascinated me. How intriguing that there was a heroism and fame which depended not on beauty, brains, strength, or even a good psychological foundation, but on willingness to surrender to love and to give love.

Reading about St. Francis of Assisi, St. Teresa of Avila, or St. Vincent de Paul, I would search for the secret of their success. Sure enough, there was always some formula which summed up each saint's way, one easy to copy until I tried to do it myself.

Even when I would give up the ideal of holiness for myself, in discouraged resignation to my ineradicable faults, I would not stop reading about these valiant souls.

Henri Bergson, the French philosopher, in his book, *The Two Sources of Morality and Religion*, claims that each saint is a new expression of God in the world. The love-energy of holy people congeals through the ages, like their plaster statues. Yet, the original inspiration was so strong that reading the life of a saint can set on fire the soul of one living centuries later.

Caryll Houselander, the English writer, evokes this image in her book, *Dry Wood*: "What people need are saints who prove in flesh and blood that they are *more* than flesh and bood."

Recently God came to me in prayer with great power. Drawn into a spiritual absorption I had not experienced before, I was eager to renew my acquaintance with my old friends, the saints. What in their writings and stories might reverberate with my own present friendship with the Lord? What could they tell me about how to navigate on a sea so inviting yet so perilous?

Within a year's time I read the lives and writings of St. Angela of Foligno, St. Catherine of Siena, St. Francis de Sales, St. Bernard of Clairvaux, St. Gertrude, St. Elizabeth Seton, Blessed Frederic Ozanam, and St. Maximilian Kolbe.

How delighted I was when something in their tales coincided with my small beginnings; but how dismayed when it seemed that sanctity could only be had at a price I was unwilling to pay. In every case I was struck by the vitality of these men and women of God.

I came to see that there was a pattern, some features common to all of the saints, whether they lived in convents, in the streets, or roamed the countryside.

Among the many such qualities, the ones that affect me the most are these: the logical consistency of the saints; the unity of their lives; their passionate love for the Lord and for the needy, based on the surprising conviction that God loved them with an intimacy hard to believe.

What is logical about the saints? Let me illustrate. Jesus, the Lord, tells us that He wants the perfection of love. No cold compromise. "The lukewarm I will spit out of My mouth." Instead of hedging about gradual growth, inevitable defects, the saint agrees with Christ that being holy, loving God with one's whole heart and one's neighbor as oneself, is really the only thing that counts. St. Francis of Assisi thought that imitating Jesus when he was on earth was the height of perfection, and so he set out in his poverty and simplicity to accomplish the most extreme lengths of that perfection.

St. Therese of Lisieux took the virtue of loving-kindness so seriously that she wouldn't allow herself so much as a moment of impatience at the myriad trifling faults of the sisters in her convent.

Convinced that one could make one's soul a cell, if deprived of a place for solitary prayer, Catherine of Siena cooked and scrubbed all day for her twenty-five brothers and sisters, not to mention the nephews, nieces, and other guests who flocked to her parents' house. Never was she heard to utter a word of complaint!

So, if each saint has a different concept of the perfection to which God calls him or her, what they have in common is the unflinching acceptance of what fidelity to that idea entails for them.

Another logical aspect of the saints is the way their belief in the eternal colors their attitudes toward passing realities.

The Marxist caricature of religion depicts the illusion of "pie in the sky when you die" operating as an opiate of the people, blunting their desire for earthly justice. Indeed, in hopeless conditions, God does want us to look forward to his supernatural promises. Would we berate lovers separated by a thousand miles for dreaming of their wedding day?

But, in fact, those whose belief in the after-life was the strongest, the saints, seemed to have had as well a tremendous desire to help others with their earthly problems.

The mystical assurance, through locutions and visions, that their own eternal happiness was guaranteed, led the saints to want to give up their own desires in sacrifice for the needs of others.

I call to mind St. Joan of Arc fearlessly enduring battle, humiliation and martyrdom for the sake of her beloved France; St. Paul enduring shipwreck, scourging and finally martyrdom to bring the message of hope to the people of his world; St. Elizabeth of Hungary, a Queen, giving away all her riches and nursing lepers in her own bed; St. Sebastian, instantly converted through the witness of a fellow soldier-martyr baring his own breast for the arrows of the persecutors in the hope of convincing them of the reality of Christ; Mother Teresa of Calcutta joyfully living in poverty to succor the dying destitute. What consummate holy logic! The way the saints made every moment meaningful, thus bringing unity to their lives, is part of their logical consistency. "Purity of heart is to will one thing," wrote Kierkegaard, the Danish theologian.

The longing for unity may seem abstract, yet it is experienced concretely by all of us, if only in the impatience we feel at the innumerable interruptions of daily existence.

On earth, of necessity, our most cherished concerns must be put aside in the pursuit of the odds and ends of life. After listening to a Bach Cantata, my next task might be to respond to a telephone salesperson offering me a discount on unwanted carpeting.

We try to bind together the diversities of life by seeking the beautiful, but we fail. Beauty is unifying, so is truth. But in the search for truth we come up against our own ignorance, by the tangled web of events beyond our deciphering.

As the Russian seekers for holiness, Tolstoy and Dostoevsky, discovered, it is only humble love that provides unity — that can make peeling a potato as significant as reading a book.

And that is what the saints knew. Unity comes from letting God, creator of heaven and earth, become the companion of our every moment, showing us His way of awe, gratitude, laughter, sorrow, yearning.

The intensity of the saints is not based on an exciting exterior life, but on openness to the God who hides eternal meaning in the hopping of a sparrow. I picture St. Maximilian

Kolbe up to all hours running his printing press in the utopian workers' village he founded in honor of Mary, Mother of God. Such care did he demonstrate for his comrades that a Communist visitor exclaimed, "Here is the only real Communism I have seen." I envisage St. Teresa of Avila doing a Spanish dance to amuse her enclosed nuns on a rainy winter afternoon. I see St. John of the Cross listening to the popular love songs the peasants sang outside his window, transposing their cadences into the lyrics of his religious poetry. There is the Cure d'Ars, not content with having heard confession for twelve hours on end in a freezing old stone church, tottering out the door to beckon to the passers-by in case they might also be secretly longing for absolution. How charming to image St. Elizabeth Seton, quarantined in a dark room outside Livorno with her dying husband, using the time when he slept to cheer a young daughter by jumping rope with her.

Thus the saints found unity through the inspiration of the Spirit of love.

The last quality of holy people to strike me is their astounding belief that God depends on them not only to do His work in the world, but also for the comfort of intimate love.

How easily we accept the cold view that God created the world on the pattern of His divine ideas or by setting up the plan of evolution, then to turn His back and leave us to our freedom. Trapped in skepticism, cynicism and despair, we find it improbable, if not impossible, to think that God could love us tenderly, constantly, with paternal and maternal affection. Coming into the mystery of the fatherhood of God was the subject of a journal workbook Sister Mary Neill, Don Briel, and I wrote called *How Shall We Find the Father?* (Seabury)

The saints, greatly influenced by the bridal imagery of the Song of Songs, knew themselves to be as cherished as a beloved spouse on her honeymoon. St. Bernard wrote that Jesus was honey in the mouth. St. Catherine describes the Lord drawing her head to his side that she might drink directly from his open heart.

The more active saints were often instructed moment by moment in prayer as to what Christ wanted of them. By day they worked, by night they rested in the arms of their God, like St. Paul, getting glimpses of what "eye has not seen, ear has not heard."

Mary, Queen of Saints, surely a woman of prayer as well as daily work, identified completely with her Son in the magnificent joy of His coming, in the suffering of His rejection and crucifixion, and finally in the glory of His Ascension, and her own Assumption into heaven. Although Mary fulfilled to perfection every quality we will explore in the other saints, we will only refer to Mary in passing in this book since Mary Neill and I have already written a book about her, entitled *Bringing the Mother With You: Healing Meditations on the Mysteries of Mary* (Seabury).

Each chapter of this book will present a brief biography of a saint, reflections by one of the authors, and then questions to elicit your own thoughts and feelings.

I would like to end this preface with a prayer:

Dear saints, companions along my way, help me to show you forth realistically so that we may take hope from your struggles. Come to us in our inner dialogue as friends, to show us how your God-given insights can become part of our lives. Most of all, through your intercession, may we experience the love of the Father, the closeness of the Son, the fire of the Holy Spirit, so that one day we may take our places with you in the everlasting kingdom of perfect joy and peace. Amen.

Acknowledgments

Selections from the following works are used by permission of the publishers.

From *Saint Francis*, by Nikos Kazantzakis, copyright © 1962 by Simon & Schuster, Inc. Reprinted by permission of Simon & Schuster, Inc.

From *Francis and Clare*, © 1982 by the Missionary Society of St. Paul the Apostle in the State of New York. Used by permission of Paulist Press.

From *Catherine of Siena: The Dialogue*, translated by Suzanne Noffke, O.P. from the Classics of Western Spirituality Series, © 1980 by the Missionary Society of St. Paul the Apostle in the State of New York. Used by permission of Paulist Press.

From *The Complete Works of St. Teresa*, translated by Allison Peers. Used with permission of Sheed & Ward, 115 E. Armour Blvd., Box 414292, Kansas City, MO 64141.

From *The Collected Works of St. Teresa of Avila*, Vol. I, translated by Kieran Kavanaugh and Otilio Rodriguez copyright, © 1976,

Table of Contents

Great Saints,
Great Friends

Mary Neill, OP *and* Ronda Chervin

ST. PAUL (c. 5 A.D. - c. 67 A.D.)

Ronda Chervin

My strongest image of St. Paul comes not from Scripture, or
Christian writing, but from a fine historical novel, *The Apostle*,
by a Jewish writer, Sholem Asch. Asch describes Paul (first
called Saul) in this way, emphasizing the Jewish intensity of his
personality:

Hearing a speech about Jesus (Yeshua) before his own
conversion, Saul "contained himself grimly and kept biting his
short fingernails. He scarcely made answer . . . it was as though
he had drawn a curtain of blackness about himself, in order that
none might see the storm that was raging in him. Tears of anger
burned on his eyelids, and he seemed to have become shorter, as
if he had shrunk in on himself. Such was the condition into
which he had been thrown by the message of the preacher . . .
finally . . . he broke out: 'But if we are to accept everything that he
says concerning Yeshua the Nazarene, we must all fall prostrate
before him, and say what was said at the foot of Sinai: "We will
do and we will obey." We must abandon all the laws of the
Torah and all that Moses taught us, and a new order of the world
will begin, the order of the Messiah. All the nations will have to

come and take upon themselves the yoke of the Kingdom of Heaven. But if this does not come to pass, then all the words that he has uttered concerning Yeshua the Nazarene are written in sand, and all those that repeat them are blasphemers of the living God; they preach apostasy, and they must be haled to judgment before the Sanhedrin.' " (Asch, pp. 32-33)

Saul was born in Tarsus about ten years after the birth of Jesus. He was a Roman citizen, though his parents were Jews. As a young man he studied in Jerusalem at the feet of the famous rabbi Gamaliel (Acts 22:3). He was a Pharisee whose great zeal for the Law led him to consider Jesus to be a false Messiah. After fiercely persecuting the early Christians, he received the famous vision of Christ on the road to Damascus. Here is Asch's description of that vision's aftermath:

"At the edge of the road lies Saul, as though a mighty hand had flung him down. About him stand his companions, paralyzed with amazement. His face is turned up to the open sky. . . . Before Saul's face stands a man. A man who is spirit and flesh and blood. He is taller than any man Saul has ever seen. Yet he is not a giant; he is an ordinary man; a Rabbi, in prayer-shawl and phylacteries; with great eyes, mournful yet radiant, filled with faith and love, eyes such as Saul has often seen among the disciples. His beard and earlocks are black, interwoven with gray. A man, not an angel; clothed in white, as for the Sabbath . . . he stretches out his hands to Saul, and the sorrow on his face is a human sorrow. His eyes are filled with tears, . . . His lips are distorted in pain, as though all the anguish of the world had passed into him. He stretches out his hands to Saul, and the unhappy voice is that of a simple man who suffers, even as Saul has seen so many suffer: 'Saul, Saul, why dost thou persecute me?' In the voice Saul hears the silent protest of all those whom he has tormented . . . 'I am Yeshua of Nazareth, whom thou persecutest.' " (Asch, p. 167)

After the vision of Jesus on the road to Damascus, Paul

withdrew into Arabia. There he did penance, and there was forged his new mission.

"The old life was one mass of sin. He had stained it with the blood of innocent men and women whose spirits had been finer, lovelier, and more godfearing than his. In the old life he had sown pain and harvested regret. The rivers of tears which he had caused to be shed, the pain he had caused to be endured, the lives he has shattered, built up a leprous growth over the whole of his first life; and there was only one cure, one salve, one healing water: faith in the Messiah. . . . Had not the lord washed him with fiery water in the baptism which he had accepted in the name of the lord? Was he not now as a new-born child which in its mother's womb had been consecrated to God as an instrument of the Messiah? . . . Whom had he to fear if he had been cleansed in the eyes of the lord, if he had been chosen as an instrument of the Messiah? . . . This faith his heart longed to bring to all men . . ." (Asch, pp. 176-177)

The rest of his life was spent as a missionary enduring great suffering from persecution as well as from hardships of travel. Division was caused by his work, for he wanted to bring the Gentiles into the Kingdom without submission to the Jewish rite of circumcision or other difficult features of the old Law.

He was probably martyred during the persecutions in Rome (A.D. 64-68).

St. Paul, such a controversial figure in his own day, is still at the center of disputes. As a professor and lecturer, I am often asked to comment on some passages in his Epistles regarded by some as definitive, and by others as outmoded. A sadness comes over me when such questions are raised, for the discussion of them seems to have obscured for many the powerful image and message of this astounding saint.

There are some characteristics of St. Paul I have always loved, others I find painful to confront, for they force me to come to grips with some of my own worst faults. I thrill to the accounts of Paul's zeal for the salvation of the world, his love of truth and willingness to die for it, his supernatural ecstasies, his endurance during trials. But when I come to such lauded passages as the famous 1 Corinthians 13:4: "love is patient, love is kind . . ." I shudder. I can imagine myself one day having faith to move mountains, but patience. . . ?

Shall I, then, one day be thrust out of the Kingdom, with Paul looking on sorrowfully shaking his head at my failure? Will I ever attain the unwearying compassion he insists upon as the hallmark of the follower of the Man who died for the sins of the world?

I will begin with the aspects of the nature of St. Paul I identify with, and then slowly work up the courage to face the rest.

Marilyn Norquist correctly describes St. Paul as a "hundred and ten percenter," a God-intoxicated man who knew but one purpose — the love of God with his whole heart and the desire to bring his neighbor to that same saving love.

We know that Paul, even before his conversion, was consumed by zeal — a burning commitment to the faith of his people in the God of Abraham, Isaac and Jacob. It was because of the strength of his love for the one, true God, that he persecuted the early followers of Jesus, considered by him to be a false Messiah. He is described as "breathing threats and murder against the disciples of the Lord." (Acts 9:1)

Only a man on fire would take the trouble to spend his days pursuing, not his own interests, but the defense of truth. Kierkegaard considered it a turning point when one ceases being concerned merely about his/her own comforts and pleasures, and seeks instead an idea to live and die for. From what we know of Paul, it seems he always had an idea to live and die for, first the God of Israel and then the Redeemer of the whole world.

The total commitment of the will was augmented in the case of Paul, by his deep sense of having been saved by a direct vision of Christ at a time when his hands were bloody with the victims of his misguided zeal. Very often the passionate love of truth is mingled with fierce pride. The defender of the faith unconsciously derives a sense of his/her own absolute worth from being linked to a perfect ideal. What is more, all the hostilities accumulated from the frustrations of existence can vent themselves in a seemingly justifiable way against the enemies of that truth.

Because I imagine Saul/Paul to have had that kind of personality, I believe he was especially touched by the figure of Jesus. Here was the Truth itself far from basking in pride, instead allowing Himself to be totally humiliated, dying the death of a slave, forgiving His enemies.

I can identify with St. Paul since I myself, a convert from a Jewish background, once scorned Christians as superstitious idiots. Not physically violent, I resorted instead to the lash of a sarcastic, ridiculing tongue. I took joy in undermining the faith of credulous fellow-students, delighting if I would see them betray their childish faith to explore the "freedom" of sin. Now I often wonder if the strong Christians among them prayed for me with the words of Jesus, as St. Stephen did for Paul: "Father, forgive them, they know not what they do."

And like St. Paul, after finding the faith, I find it most difficult to have compassion on those who, as I did in the past, have no interest in hearing the message of salvation. I want them to convert immediately and to be ready to live and die for the faith.

A poem, published in the *El Playano* (Loyola Marymount University, 1983), expressed my feelings of impatience with those who cannot sympathize with my zealous ways:

JEWISH CONVERT

Lured by shining
riches of their land,
undocumented, led by saints,
I made my way one night,
under the barbed wire
of ancient prejudice.

Clothing wet with
sweat and tears,
tongued betraying
my origins,
how could I pass?

Then, camouflaged
in free yet costly
garb of Your mysteries
I worked for what they
thought were lowest wages,
but to me seemed glorious wealth.

For some of them
had lost the dream,
for which I risked my life.
My eagerness they scorned,
as I sewed my citizenship papers
in the pocket of my heart.

Yet patience must not become that phony tolerance
bespeaking a luke-warm faith. Never does God the Father, or the
Son, or the Spirit, or the saints, tell us that it does not matter
what we believe, that all will be well, regardless. No. Did Christ
die to propagate a weak humanism?

And so there is a battle within me. The false zeal of Saul

bids me wipe out the enemies of holy truth lest these wolves destroy the sheep — those of the flock who cannot defend themselves against error. Then, upset at the anger such a stance evokes, I long to run away from the mission, to hide in a back pew of the Church with my truth.

I hear the spirit of St. Paul calling out to me — *"preach the truth in love."* You must preach the word in season and out of season, fighting the good fight and keeping the faith (1 Timothy 12) but not like a clanging cymbal (1 Corinthians 14); rather with a heart full of love for Christ and for the people He died to save.

And Paul shows us how this is to be done. First of all, we are to open ourselves by telling our own story, no matter how shameful. Over and over again whenever we read of St. Paul coming to a new city, he recounts his sins by way of introduction.

So often I find, in teaching or lecturing, that it is only when I take a risk and let the group in on my own struggles and sufferings that they are willing to hear about the ways God has helped me.

What is more, we must not subtly flee from our passion and His Passion by making of the faith a cool philosophical doctrine. "But the Messiah was not a symbol or a series of symbols; he was not a 'philosophy,' or wisdom. . . . The Messiah was and is the flesh and blood of faith for all, the universal redemption. Every man is buried with the Messiah and every man is resurrected with him through faith in the work of God. In the faith every man shares the triumph of the Messiah over death, not symbolically, but in the flesh." (Asch, p. 636)

As a philosophy student before my conversion, I loved the search for intellectual truth. Then I realized that the mind alone leads to skepticism. Meeting Catholic philosophers, I found that they could refute skepticism with their superior minds, but that still left a void. Suppose there was truth, what did it profit me to be absolutely sure that 2 plus 2 equals 4, or even to find an air-tight proof for the existence of a God who had no face?

And so coming for the first time upon Paul's words, "The wisdom of the world is foolishness," I dimly understood that there was an abyss between the conceptual God and the God of love my Catholic friends worshipped. After finding "God the Father of Our Lord Jesus Christ," my soul reverberated to the words of the great convert — Pascal:

> Fire, fire, fire. . . .
> Not the God of the philosophers, the living God, the God of Abraham, Isaac, and Jacob. Tears, tears . . . tears of joy.

And now, as a teacher of Christian philosophy, I struggle with the problem of trying to show how the truth of the mind opens us to faith, ever aware that even in the process, my very tone of voice might give the impression that God is only a concept. I invite the students on retreats where I can break out of the schoolroom inhibitions and witness more directly my experience of God's love. Afterwards I am exhausted but happy. I have been real. With the help of the members of my retreat team, and the grace of God, we have opened them to hope in a God who might assuage their own most profound longings.

It is hard afterwards to come back to the stiffer atmosphere of philosophical deliberation. And yet, these same students would not go on a retreat were they not first approached with a conceptual formulation of the meaning of faith and experience as ways of coming to new knowledge.

And so I beg St. Paul to intercede for me in my weariness — to help me to believe that if I do my part in plowing the earth and planting the seed his God and mine will bring in the harvest.

Reading the account of St. Paul's life given in Acts and in his Epistles, I am also impressed by the fact that never did the saint rely on human wisdom and eloquence but instead on the Holy Spirit and the supernatural gifts that the Spirit brought. (1 Thessalonians 1:5)

Paul's original conversion was by means of a vision. The acceptance of the Gentiles without circumcision was largely based on the fact that they had received the Spirit. How was this known? Because they prayed in tongues. (Acts 11:45; Acts 15:8) When Paul's words of truth were rejected by Gentiles it was through miracles that they were convinced. When the Church was on the verge of splitting over doctrinal matters it was through visions that Peter the first of the Apostles was instructed.

Only a man with the strong life of incessant prayer that Paul himself recommended, could have endured all the trials he describes in one of his most comforting passages, "For I am sure that neither death, nor life, nor angels, nor principalities, nor things present, nor things to come, nor powers, nor height, nor depth, nor anything else in all creation, will be able to separate us from the love of God in Christ Jesus our Lord." (Romans 8:38) And this from a man who had suffered scourging, stoning, imprisonment, hunger, shipwreck.

"And when they had inflicted many blows upon them (Paul and Silas) they threw them into prison . . . fastened their feet in the stocks. But about midnight Paul and Silas were praying and singing hymns to God. . . ." (Acts 16:25)

And so it is still with those now being persecuted for Christ. If they call upon the name of the Lord they are given amazing graces to fortify them in the most unbearable conditions. The modern example most vivid in my mind is that of Richard Wurmbrand the Rumanian Lutheran pastor, also a Jewish convert, who was thrown into Communist prisons for more than a decade. A man of immense activities in the intellectual and missionary fields, he immediately sought to convert all those in his cell, as well as the jailers. Many times the torturers, due to a change in administration, were themselves hurled into the cells among those they had formerly beaten. Wurmbrand insisted that the prisoners show merciful forgiveness to their enemies, and in this way brought many Communists into the experience of the merciful love of Christ.

Aware of the bad effects of Wurmbrand's prison ministry, the authorities put him into solitary confinement for several years. Unable to exercise his usual talents for conversation, he began for the first time to practice deep interior prayer. Often his guards would find this starving prisoner, just like Paul and Silas, singing hymns to God and dancing around his cell in his chains. His faithful wife, who kept her marriage vows even though she was continually being told falsely that her husband had perished in the jail, was herself finally sent to prison camp. Put into a tiny closet with nails digging into her skin, she suddenly became ecstatic and realized that she had received the gift of tongues.

How shall those of us who have never had a hair on our heads disturbed by physical persecution relate to such examples? My experience is that mental pain is just as terrible as bodily suffering. In either case we are given the choice of becoming bitter with anger at our fate, or of courageously flinging ourselves into the arms of God and letting Him console us.

"But does He always console us?" you might be asking. I believe that He does, though not always in the manner and time that we wish. Often we beg for a cessation of pain, but He wants for us peace in the midst of pain. In our anguish, when the immediate suffering is not removed, we may push away the offer of peace. Often, we want an immediate removal of the cause of our psychological misery, but He wants for us a true reconciliation. In our resentment, we ignore the openings grace is making for healing.

And so again I ask St. Paul to help me. "Great staunch saint of God, here I am your puny admirer — one who can hardly stand a pinprick or a yawn. I do not ask you to toughen me, as if we were stoics, but rather to turn me in hope toward the source of all help, 'the Father who comforts us in all our afflictions.' " (2 Corinthians 1:4)

It is only when we experience comfort from God directly or through others who minister this to us in friendship that we are able to come to that virtue of compassion, the consideration of which I have saved until the end.

How is it that we are so eager to win from others their understanding of our foibles, yet so harsh in our judgments of them? "Why do you look at the mote in your brother's eye and ignore the beam in your own?" Jesus admonished us. We are not to judge even the worst sins for there is nothing unforgivable to God, save the refusal of forgiveness, over which He has no power.

And so Paul, the most Jewish of Jews, came to love the Gentiles even though most of them were sunken in sin. Sholem Asch describes Paul watching pagan rites, and then explaining to his friends what love this sight engendered in him;

" 'The world is carried away by a flood of abomination! Men have become worse than the beasts of the field in their fleshy lusts. They squirm like vermin in the filth of their whoredom. . . . This would be the end if God had not taken pity on the world of mankind and sent it His Messiah, to cleanse it in his baptism and to bring it under the yoke of the Kingdom of Heaven. I hear the voice of the lord calling to me: "Take pity on these people, and bring them the tidings of my advent. Carry the news from end to end of the world, so that there shall not be under the heavens a single people which has not heard the name of the one living God and of the Messiah whom He sent, a comfort and a salvation for man.' Bar Naba stared at his friend. He recognized the old, passionate zeal; once it had burned in hatred, but now it burned in love and devotion to the man of sorrow." (Asch, p. 284)

For me compassion comes most often through the mediation of psychological insight. When I stare at the faults of others I am disgusted and repelled; but then if I get a chance to penetrate into the wounds which led to the negative behavior, I am less judging. If, even for a moment, the throbbing heart of the other becomes visible, then I am opened to compassion.

And so I end this chapter with another appeal to my beloved St. Paul:

You who could forgive your kinsmen for scorning you, the Romans for scourging you, and even God for depriving you of the sight of the earthly victory of your cause, ask the Father of compassion to melt my heart. May I, like you, have but one goal, that all may find the love of the Father which is in Christ Jesus.

FOR PERSONAL REFLECTION

1. What aspects of Paul's character and mission do you identify with especially?

2. Would you describe yourself as zealous now or in the past? What are some instances in your life of harmful zeal? Have you ever been the victim of someone else's fanaticism? What of good zeal — can you give credit to others for positive zealousness even if it is challenging to you?

3. How do you feel about personal witness? Can you receive it from others? Are you free to give it yourself? What fears do you have about self-revelation in religious matters? Of these fears, which do you think are justified, and which are obstacles to communication?

4. How do you respond to philosophical and theological presentations of the truths about God? Do you find them stimulating or cold?

5. What gifts of the Spirit are real in your life? Read 1 Corinthians 12:4-11 and see which ones you might want to pray for.

6. How have you found consolation in trial?

7. When have you experienced compassion? Who is in need of your understanding now?

ST. FRANCIS of ASSISI (1181-1226)

Ronda Chervin

There is a certain difficulty in writing about St. Francis of Assisi. He is so well-known, so beloved, he belongs to all of us so profoundly. How can one introduce someone so familiar?

And yet, in the case of all the very popular saints, we always want to find a way to come closer to them. Like favorite flavors of ice-cream, we never tire of savoring them.

Over and again we want to hear about this medieval saint (1181-1226), the son of a rich merchant, who, wounded in battle came to realize the evil of his previous dilettante lifestyle, was moved to embrace a life of complete poverty in the footsteps of his beloved Lord Jesus, preached to the people and even to the animals, formed an order of mendicant brothers and sisters and other followers, and died with the sacred wounds of Christ in his own body.

My experience of St. Francis began on a trip to Assisi. It was 1959. I was not yet a Catholic but was nearing that decision. In a tourist bus filled with lovers of Catholic art, I came upon the birthplace of the saint of Umbria.

It was twilight when we arrived in the square. Everyone was hoping that the cathedral would still be open.

The upper stories of the building were dark, mysterious and warm, the inner walls decorated with famous frescoes; but it was the crypt, still darker, candle-lit, which moved me to tears and awe. My prayer-life was but one-day-old, for the night before, in Pisa, I had knelt for the first time, uttering the skeptic's prayer self-consciously — "God, if there is a God, let me know it." The small underground crypt of the Church of Assisi has that same cave-like, round, low-ceilinged style to be found in the Franciscan sanctuaries throughout Italy. The smallness was because of the tiny stature of St. Francis. It was small enough to make touching the wall inviting, also making it more natural to kneel or crouch, than to stand erect. In the sacred womb of its enclosure I felt safe, loved. I wanted to stay forever.

Years later, when my husband and I resided in Italy, we used to drive up occasionally on weekends to see the Franciscan shrine nearest to Rome — Fonte Columbo and Greccio. Regardless of the hour, there would always be some visitors to these out of the way places. The patient friar guides would form us into a group and take us through. I would let the others move ahead, and once alone in some tiny room built by the early brothers with their own hands, I would lie on the ground and kiss the stones, rising very quickly to avoid attracting attention. How ashamed I would be of caring so much about appearances. St. Francis did much more outlandish things in public without fear. If I loved him so, why wouldn't I welcome ridicule, as he did?

My favorite pictures of Francis are not the famous ones of Giotto which I have always found a bit austere, but rather the Cimabue fresco of the older St. Francis. I love, as well, a less well-known panel showing the tiny form of Francis wiping away his tears with a large handkerchief. I have read many biographies of the saint. Chesterton's *St. Francis* delighted me intellectually. Bonaventure's beautiful story of the life of his Master was the most spiritually pure. *The Fioretti*, better known as *The Little Flowers of St. Francis*, a collection of anecdotes collected by the brothers of his own days are the most charming. But the rendition with the strongest image for me is that of Nikos Kazantzakis in his novel *Saint Francis*.

The author of *Zorba the Greek*, Kazantzakis was a maverick mystic who loved Christ and the saint but never was able to make his own peace with the Greek Orthodox Church or with the God he adored, yet wrestled with to his death.

Burning with a passionate desire to become like St. Francis, Kazantzakis gives one of the most exciting portrayals of our hero. The book is written as if penned by Brother Leo, St. Francis' constant companion, depicted by Kazantzakis as a sort of Sancho Panza. Here are some characteristic excerpts:

"As far as I can gauge his height in my mind, I can say only this with certitude: from the ground trodden by his feet, from there to his head, his stature was short; but from the head upward it was immense." (Kazantzakis, p. 27)

"When Francis was among men he would laugh and frolic — would spring suddenly into the air and begin to dance, or would seize two sticks and play the 'viol' while singing sacred songs he himself had composed. Doubtlessly he did so to encourage his companions, realizing perfectly well that the soul suffers, the body hungers, and man's endurance is nil. When he was alone, however, his tears began to flow. He would beat his chest, roll in the thorns and nettles, lift his hands to heaven and cry. 'All day long I search for Thee desperately, Lord; all night long while I am asleep Thou searchest for me. O Lord, when, as night gives way to day, shall we meet?' " (Kazantzakis, p. 28)

"Place your trust in man's soul, Brother Leo, and do not listen to the advice of prudence. The soul can achieve the impossible . . . open your mind and engrave deeply there what I am about to tell you. The body of man is the bow, God is the archer, and the soul is the arrow. Understand? . . .

"What I mean, Brother Leo, is this: There are three kinds of prayer:

"The first: 'Lord, bend me, or else I shall rot.'

"The second: 'Lord, do not bend me too much, for I shall break.'

"The third, Brother Leo, is our prayer: 'Lord, bend me too much, and who cares if I break!' " (Kazantzakis, pp. 178-179)

"Hearing much chirping above him, he looked up. 'Stay where you are, Brother Leo . . . Don't move; you might frighten them. Since I haven't any grain to throw them, I shall feed them with the word of God so that they may hear it and be able, like men, to go to heaven.'

"Turning to the birds, he leaned over them and began to preach, his arms spread wide.

" 'Sister Birds, God, the Father of birds and men, loves you greatly, and you are aware of this. That is why when you drink water you lift your tiny heads to heaven after each sip and give thanks to Him; why in the morning when the sun strikes your little breasts you fill yourselves with song and fly from branch to branch glorifying His name, the name of the Lord, who sends the sun, and green trees, and song. And you fly high up into the sky so that you can come close to Him and He can hear you. And when your nests are filled with eggs and you are mothers sitting on them to hatch them, God becomes a male bird, sits Himself down on the branch opposite, and sings to ease your labors.'

"Francis leaned further and further forward. He kept shaking his robe as though it were a pair of wings, and his voice chirruped, sweet as a nightingale's . . . ." (Kazantzakis, pp. 189-190)

Addressing Sister Clare and her companions:

"Struggle and more struggle, my sisters, ascent along the uphill road, extreme suffering; and purity, love, poverty, hunger, nakedness, tears — all these are required! Satan has laid his snares everywhere; they are just waiting for us to fall in. If you bend down to smell a flower, my sisters, you will find him there; if you lift a stone he will be hidden beneath and waiting. . . .

What is he waiting for? For our souls to become momentarily fatigued and drowsy, for the instant when they cease to stand as our ever-vigilant sentinels, and thus enable him to leap on us and drag us down into hell. My sisters, you are the ones I am thinking of, the ones I pity — much more than the men; because you are women, and your hearts do not steel themselves easily. . . ." (Kazantzakis, p. 250)

"What happiness it is, . . . what joy not to have any will, not to say 'I,' but to forget who you are, what your name is, and to give yourself up with confidence to the puffs of God's wind! That is true freedom! If someone asks you who is free, Brother Leo, what will you reply? The man who is God's slave! All other freedom is bondage." (Kazantzakis, p. 273)

Such Franciscan themes embellished by Kazantzakis' dramatic prose should not overshadow the actual words of the saint spoken during his pilgrimage. Recently, Paulist Press has included the complete works of St. Francis in a volume entitled *Francis and Clare* as part of their Classics of Western Spirituality series.

I suggest you read slowly these excerpts from the famous *Canticle of the Sun*:

> Most High, all-powerful, good Lord,
> Yours are the praises, the glory, the honor,
> and all blessing.
> To you alone, Most High, do they belong,
> and no man is worthy to mention Your name.
>
> Praised be You, my Lord, with all your creatures,
> especially Sir Brother Sun,
> Who is the day and through whom
> You give us light
> And he is beautiful and radiant with
> great splendor;
> and bears a likeness of You, Most High One.

Praised be You, my Lord, through Sister Moon and
the stars,
in heaven You formed them clear and precious and
beautiful. . . .

Praised be You, my Lord, through Sister Water,
which is very useful and humble and precious and
chaste.

Praised be You, my Lord, through Brother Fire,
through whom You light the night
and he is beautiful and playful and robust and
strong.

Praised be You, my Lord, through our
Sister Mother Earth,
who sustains and governs us,
and who produces varied fruits with colored
flowers and herbs.

Praised be You, my Lord, through our
Sister Bodily Death,
from whom no man can escape.
Woe to those who die in mortal sin.
Blessed are those whom death will find in Your
most holy will,
for the second death shall do them no harm.
Praise and bless my Lord and give Him thanks
and serve Him with great humility.

(*Francis and Clare*, pp. 38-39)

You might want to pause here and make your own list of
favorite creatures calling them brother and sister.

Seeing the glory of God in nature is certainly not original
with St. Francis. We read it in the Psalms. But then we may ask,

how is it that so many read those Psalms daily and yet seldom take them to heart, rarely allow themselves to exult in joy in the glory of God in beauty to the extent that St. Francis rejoiced?

I, myself, was very slow to discover the beauty of the created world. A city girl from the middle of metropolitan New York, it was the shining electric lights deep underground seen from a subway car, that first attracted my attention. Only in my twenties was I opened to the exquisiteness of natural beauty: first trees, then mountains, then oceans, then flowers.

An artist friend of mine, Kathy Hall, much influenced by St. Francis likes to speak of the varied hues of nature as "His colors." One day this mystery opened itself to me in a new way. I was walking on the beach when the words came to me "This is Me as an ocean." "This is Me as a bird." "This is Me as blue." The glorious litany ended with the startling perception, "You are Me as Ronda."

My experience indicates that fresh words can open us to a perennial experience. And so it must have been in the time of St. Francis. Calling water "Sister Water" and fire "Brother Fire," and death "Sister Death," released a flood of delight in the hearts of the men and women who heard the saint's song.

My favorite scene from the film, *Brother Sun, Sister Moon*, is that of young Francis, freed from the atmosphere of commerce, running through the field of poppies. The movie has its limitations, but has enough charm to make up for them, I believe.

"Less is more" states a slogan popular at the time of this writing. Besides associating Francis with joy in beauty, we also think of him as the saint of simplicity — called by him, paradoxically, *Lady* Poverty.

The Franciscan ideal of poverty has an appeal, not only to those who decide to don the brown robe and live his way of life, but also for middle-class people such as myself, appalled by the clutter of our well-furnished houses, dreaming of freedom from worldly cares, haunted by the notion of one day throwing off our bourgeois trappings and living in the forests.

Francis and others of his era very suddenly decided to give it all up for the joy of simplicity. They were ready to brave not only the ridicule of their relatives and friends, but also the harshness of the elements, if only they might be liberated to a new life.

In my case, it is a matter of slowly divesting myself of blind attachment to innumerable habits blocking the way to greater appreciation of the gifts of nature. One year, I realized that it would be much more pleasant to travel light than to lug huge, heavy suitcases around the world. On a three week trip to the Holy Land, I decided to limit my baggage to whatever would fit in one back-pack. It worked! Three wrap-skirts, three blouses, one dress, one slip, and a few changes of underwear, plus a large sweater turned out to be quite enough.

On the way, I bought one dress more, and tried to discard the old one. This attempt turned out to be humorous. I left the discarded dress on top of a garbage can with the idea that some poor person might find it happily and take it away. When I returned to the room, there it was again. My husband had found it and "saved" it for me!

It was a great delight to be free of the burden of suitcases in Israel and also to spend less time deciding what to wear. Since then, I have been more diligent in cleaning out closets. The process involves a healthy sense of individuality for me. What I give away are usually garments I had picked up, not because I loved them as expressing some style consonant with my own personality, but rather, clothing chosen to fit into a role.

Another form of simplicity and relative poverty for me has been the adoption of natural foods over processed and frozen edibles. Before adopting this cooking style, I selected food exclusively in terms of what appealed to my taste-buds, with no thought of nutritional value. This resulted in a heavy, stuffed feeling after meals since my favorites are bacon, cheese, and chocolate cake. I still indulge in these occasionally, but it was a new experience for me to discover that when vegetables become stars in a dinner (instead of optional extras) it is wonderful to savor their colors, their forms, and their fresh taste.

My latest attempt at simplicity has been to do without a car (something of a major project in a city such as Los Angeles with very inadequate surface transport). Relegating errands to my husband, who is better at dealing with the external world anyhow, and leaving the home tasks to myself, I found that my only necessary trips were to the university and the church, both of which are a mere ten blocks away.

You might think it would be very easy to choose to walk rather than drive, especially in sunny southern California; and yet, it was a hard decision. Would I, weak, lazy, unathletic have the courage to walk even on days when it was too warm, too rainy, or when I felt otherwise under the weather? But under the influence of so much reading about St. Francis, I finally made the decision. I put my car on the market, strapped my Birkenstocks to my bare feet and started off, singing alleluia and feeling Franciscan at last.

After about three months into my walking life, we sold the house and moved to the ocean, too far to walk. I started on the bus. Then I was offered a job as a consultant to a new Catholic TV station based 45 miles away. The evangelistic possibilities of the TV job seemed to me more important than not owning a car. However, the memory of that greater simplicity of car-less freedom remains, and now that I am no longer at the TV station, the dream is returning.

Of course St. Francis was not only interested in liberating himself through holy poverty, but also in being close to those poor, not by choice, but by necessity. He wanted to prove to them their dignity in the eyes of God by his own identification with their troubles. He wanted to show them how to praise God in any circumstance. He also took pleasure in giving away his riches and seeing his followers do the same.

There are at least two main ways of imitating St. Francis in compassion for the poor. One is by working with the needy directly. How much I admire those who run soup-kitchens, take the destitute off the streets, visit convalescent homes, or participate in any of the other fine programs for relieving the suffering of others. Yet, I have a horror of doing this. St. Francis underwent one of the most important moments of conversion when he obeyed Christ who told him to kiss a leper.

Brought up in a family of intellectuals, and very healthy ones at that, I was never taught to admire corporal works of mercy. What counted much more was to do something creative, original, interesting. Adding the spirit to the intellect, after my conversion, gave me still another way to escape from the material exigencies of life. The necessity of immersing myself in the physical world in the form of changing diapers or wiping little mouths dripping with baby food was endured only because I could distract myself with the beauty of the faces and forms of the babies.

Preparing food is redeemed by the delicious results, and sex can be experienced as an overflow of love; but what of tending the elderly sick? What can redeem such tasks? Only love. Alas, how little pure compassion there is in me!

And so I pray, St. Francis, you who kissed the wounds of lepers, seeing Christ Himself in their rotting flesh, beg for me the lesser grace of being ready to serve my loved ones, or anyone whom God sends, in their dire bodily needs. Let me be afraid of nothing which God might will for me.

Almost as a substitute for the willingness to perform corporal works of mercy, I have become totally committed to the idea of tithing to support those who *do* take care of "the poorest of the poor." This practice has given me much relief, for indeed I do care terribly about the destitute and cannot bear to think of someone lying homeless on a cold pavement while I snuggle under my electric blanket. My dream is that one day I will be in a position to give much more than ten percent of my income to the poor, that in the future when I do not have to balance my own desires in this regard with the legitimate needs of family members, I may be able to live in real simplicity and give all the rest to the needy. May this great wish come to fruition through the intecession of you, my saint, Francis.

Detachment, struggle, sweat, tears! These were very much a part of the life of St. Francis.

St. Francis wept first of all because he, himself, found it so difficult to persevere toward the goal of imitating Christ. There were the sins of the flesh engrained in his body and soul from the habits of the past, what we would now call the shadow self.

At any moment Francis could have abandoned the life of poverty, fled from his cold caves with only a rock for a pillow, to return to his father's rich house, to marry some charming young woman replete with dowry. At moments of ecstasy when the Holy Spirit swooped into his soul to fill it with bliss, there was no question but that he had made the better choice. But what about the other times — the moments when all he had was the hunger, the cold, and worst of all the knowledge that many of his brothers had already, within his own lifetime, betrayed their promises and worked out an easier rule?

There were other reasons for tears. Reading the authentic writings of Francis, it is clearly brought out how much he was a son of the Church. The film *Brother Sun, Sister Moon* can leave the impression that Francis set up an alternate religious life with prayer-meetings instead of the Mass, spontaneous songs instead of the breviary, free brothers and sisters with no priests. But such was not the case. As the documents show, Francis loved the Eucharist, receiving it daily (*Francis and Clare*, p. 50), ordered his followers to pray regularly, and revered the priesthood. Yet he wept for the Church — for the negligent priests, for the self-indulgent laity.

Burning with love for Christ, for the Blessed Sacrament, for the Virgin Mary, how could he not suffer to the depth of his soul to see the offer of love from the Savior scorned?

I recall being horrified by the words of a friar at a Franciscan sanctuary. Oohing and ahhing about the joyful spirit of St. Francis, I was rudely interrupted when the guide remarked sharply, "We who stay here come, not for the scenic view, but to do penance."

How could it be otherwise? Francis wanted to follow in the footprints of Christ. Yes, there are Christ's words about the lilies of the fields and the birds of the air, to let us glimpse the exultation of the Lord in the Father's creation, but most of the life of Jesus was permeated by suffering — infinite sorrow because of the hell God's favorite creatures had made of His world, tremendous empathy for the poor, ground under the heel of the rich, and for the rich, too, so tight with greed they could not appreciate the things of God.

And so I pray "Dear Jesus, give me the courage to weep the way St. Francis did. Pierce me with Your wounds and let flow out blood and water, lest I become congealed in stoic resignation, seeking escape in foolish comforts, fleeing Your pain and thus losing the chance to receive Your comfort, Your hope."

Let us pray together the words St. Francis put at the end of his Rule (*Francis and Clare*, pp. 131-134)

> All-powerful, most holy, most high and
> supreme God. . . .
>
> You have created all things spiritual and corporal
> and, having made us *in Your own image and likeness,*
> You placed us in paradise.
> And through our own fault we have fallen. . . .

and You willed to redeem us captives
through His cross and blood and death.

And we thank You
for Your Son Himself will come again
in the glory of His majesty
to send the wicked ones
who have not done penance and
who have not known You
into the eternal fire,
and to say to all those who have known You
and have adored You
and have served You in penance:
'Come, you blessed of my Father,
receive the kingdom. . . .'

Let all of us
wherever we are
in every place
at every hour
at every time of day
everyday and continually
believe truly and humbly
and keep in our heart
and love, honor, adore, serve
praise and bless
glorify and exalt
magnify and give thanks to
the most high and supreme eternal God

Who is
without beginning and without end
unchangeable, invisible,
indescribable, ineffable,
incomprehensible, unfathomable,

blessed, worthy of praise,
glorious, exalted on high, sublime,
most high, gentle, lovable,
delectable, and totally desirable above all else
forever.
Amen.

FOR PERSONAL REFLECTION

1. What do you like best about St. Francis?   What challenges you?
2. Which of the three kinds of prayers that Kazantzakis had St. Francis propose is the closest to your own:
   Lord, bend me or else I shall rot!
   Lord, do not bend me too much, for I shall break!
   Lord, bend me too much, and who cares if I break!
3. Go through a day calling each thing brother or sister and write the highlights of your own hymn of praise.
4. What have been your experiments with simplicity?   Make a list of the material goods you could live with minimally.
5. How do you show care for the poor?
6. Who are the lepers in your life?
7. Do you allow yourself to weep for your own sufferings and those of others?

ST. THOMAS AQUINAS (1225-1274)

Mary Neill

Thomas Aquinas, unlike other saints of more engaging or dramatic personalities, takes time to appreciate, separated as we are from him by the distance of years, and the fossilization of the man behind the prodigious work and system of Thomism.

I was lucky to be introduced to Thomas as a novice by a young Dominican priest, the late Father Joseph Servente, who would open the *Summa* and speak passionately of the meaning of St. Thomas. Because Fr. Joe Servente loved Thomas, he brought to life what could have been a dead system. Reading from the *Canticle of Canticles* on which Thomas commented as he lay dying, this young Italian priest exemplified a theology that was not divorced from spirituality. I still have a copy of the *Summa* I received in the novitiate as a gift.

St. Thomas was presented to us in the novitiate, too, as a model of chastity. We were given to wear the medal depicting his being girded by an angel about the waist after his brothers had tried to sway him from his vocation by sending a prostitute to the room where they had imprisoned him. The usually phlegmatic Thomas, the story goes, had chased her out of his room with a log snatched from the fireplace — some indication

that the fires of the flesh could be contained only by other kinds
of fire. We used to joke about the story and about having to wear
the "chastity belt." Later, life would teach me indeed that only
fire can fight fire: that it is the "No," that makes a genuine "Yes"
possible. In our times, when chastity itself in all forms seems a
joke, Thomas offers a powerful comment on the relationship
between the passion of the mind and the passions of the flesh.

When I was studying for my Master's degree in religion, I
was taught principally by Thomists: some good, and some bad.
The good teachers used Thomas imaginatively and creatively;
the poor teachers used him as a security and held that Thomas
had given all the answers for all time. For some years I felt
cheated by the lacunae left in my theological education by its
concentration on Thomas. Yet, when I came to do doctoral work
in France, I was grateful for the way Thomistic method had
taught me to think. He always trusted objections and put them
right out front; he honored and dialogued with traditional
thought, but was not enslaved to it. His thought was spacious,
balanced and graceful like the Gothic architecture constructed
around the same time he built his theological edifice.

In the years of teaching in the Bay Area, my respect for the
profound rationalism of the Church, which has declared
Thomas its prince of theologians, has grown as I have seen the
damage done by some liberals who trust that feelings are infallible guardians of truth in a way that thinking is not; by some
people I have met who were severly scarred by turning their lives
over either to an Eastern guru or to a fundamentalist Christian
who trained them to distrust their own thought and never to
question.

Further study and interest in mysticism has also renewed
my appreciation of the profound prayer life of St. Thomas, his
illuminations and the beauty of the poetry that flowed from his
pen in the hymns he composed for Corpus Christi. Long before I
had known Thomas was their author, I had grown to love the

Pange Lingua, the *Tantum Ergo;* the *Adoro Te devote, Latens Deitas* that I had so often sung as a Catholic school child at benediction or in processions. Thomas — poet, mystic, writer: powerful combination. *Latens Deitas:* what a beautiful description of God — *latens,* hidden godliness in the Eucharist that is the Mass of the Church, in the graciousness of God, latent in all the world.

One summer, pondering again the frescoes painted in the San Marco convent in Florence by the Dominican Fra Angelico not long after Thomas' death, I was struck again by his picture of St. Thomas gazing at the crucified Lord. Others weep; this gentle giant, this hulk of a man, stands at a distance, eyes open, trying to see to understand, caught in an undertone deeper than feeling. If we become what we gaze at, the Godliness that Thomas contemplates shines from his face and from his work.

It was inevitable, perhaps, for me to become interested in Jungian thought after I had been steeped in Thomas for so many years. First, because Jung had great respect for the medieval mind as the source of our modern consciousness. He studied medieval alchemy when others scorned it, for he saw that in the middle ages the inner and the outer, the scientific and the spiritual had not yet been separated, so that clues for healing the deep split within the modern psyche may be found there. (What a provocative idea: for some theologian to study Thomas in this creative Jungian way.) Jung felt too that the marriage of opposites within us (patterned in the marriage of God-Man which Christ exemplifies) is the antidote to the endemic fear and violence of our time, where we are always seeking to disown or even kill some "opposite" theory, or feeling or creed or person.

Thomas is a saint because he married so many opposites within himself:

1. He married Aristotelian thought to theology, an extremely dangerous thing at the time, for which he was

condemned by many. Reason and faith, thought opposites in many ways, he showed could be united in a creative dialogue.

2. Though he came from royalty, he embraced a profound poverty in becoming a mendicant Dominican; he had to tramp all over Europe by foot: Naples to Rome to Paris to Cologne and then back, always begging food. Try it; you won't like it — it's hard enough by car.

3. He combined the profound elitism of a piercing intellect with great humility — many legends point to his simplicity that was mistaken for stupidity.

4. He combined being a wonderful scholar with being an exciting teacher and preacher. Audiences were known to weep or to burst into applause during his sermons. Seeing profoundly and being able to communicate what you see clearly are two very separate skills, not often found in the same person.

5. He combined the political and the academic. He was always being asked to give counsel to popes and kings and to the General Chapters of his Dominican Order — and he had to resist offers of political power as cardinal or abbot. Yet he was able to pass back into the humdrum of daily writing and teaching.

Radical, yet respectful of tradition; royaly born, yet poor; intellectual yet compassionate; political, yet withdrawn from the world; brilliant yet humble; Thomas models for us the hope that we can suffer the conflict of our own opposites in such a way that life and love and grace may flow from this.

Let us now look at the stepping stones of his life in more detail to savor this unusual man.

Thomas, whose name aptly means abyss, was one of six children born in the Aquinas family, related by blood to Emperor Frederick II of Sicily and to St. Louis IX of France. His godfather was Pope Honorius, and Thomas was early on expected to become a churchman of great power and influence as his older brothers were secular lords. Lovely legends surround his childhood — that he organized his mother's papers in a family chest he crawled to; that he tried to eat a parchment that had *Ave Maria* printed on it; that when a child of five, he was sent to study at the Abbey of Monte Cassino, and kept asking, "*What* is God?" rather than the more proper, "Who is God?" and would not change the question. His infant sister was killed by lightning in the place where they both lay, and ever after in his life he was frightened by lightning and used to run and comfort himself by the tabernacle, even as a grown man.

After being educated at Monte Cassino as a child, he went at fourteen to the University of Naples where he was obviously a brilliant student (later he would hide this brilliance) and where he became enamored with the Dominicans he met there, asking to enter their Order when he was seventeen. They suggested he wait a year, accurately anticipating the explosion that would come from the family when they heard that their son, slated in their minds to head the wealthy Monte Cassino, wanted to become a beggar in an Order, "socially unacceptable," founded only in 1216.

After his father died in 1244 Thomas entered the Dominican Convent in Naples, but within the year was kidnapped by his brothers at the order of his enraged mother, Theodora. Stoically resisting his passionate mother's pleas, he was kept imprisoned in the family castle for a year and visited only by his two sisters who were to try to bring him to his senses. Thomas got books from the convent in Naples, resisted his brothers' intrusion, mollified his sisters and ultimately got their help in escaping. Finally, he had to plead his case before the pope against his family. Innocent IV tried to effect a compromise: Thomas could be both a Dominican and head of Monte Cassino. Thomas refused. It takes considerable courage and maturity for an eighteen-year-old to resist his culture and family in such a way; Thomas' inner sense of self grounded in God must have been strong early on. His family was simply unfair to him, but he resisted their intrusions stubbornly. His gentleness was not to be mistaken for weakness.

The next years of Thomas' life were given over to intense study among the 20,000 students at Paris, the heart of France, where the present lovely cathedral of Notre Dame had just been built. Living at the Dominican Convent of St. James, which his cousin St. Louis of France helped repair, Thomas began a lifelong friendship with St. Albert the Great who early on saw Thomas' genius, though at this time Thomas had become silent ("taciturn") and was often mistaken as slow and stupid, hence his nickname, "The Dumb Ox."

Albert, living in the cell next to Thomas, devoted himself to guiding Thomas and even, according to legend, set up a public debate between himself and Thomas so that his student's brilliance could be better seen. In these years Thomas studied in Cologne, was ordained, became a lecturer at the University of Paris, took his B.A. at 27 (though it was not usually conferred until 35) and met another brother, Reginald, who became his confessor, spiritual director and friend.

Thomas was a popular teacher — his classes had to be held out in the open. And his daring introduction of Aristotle into theological discourse, his courage in questioning the traditional sources of theological insight — Augustine, Dionysius, Ambrose and Basil as well as his obtaining one of the coveted chairs of the university made him disliked and envied not only by other clerics but by some of his own Dominican brothers.

He had a tremendous capacity for work, was affable and gentle, ready to help anybody at any time, whether within the convent or without. No one held him in awe or fear. No one who knew him disliked him. He was not an ordinary man, but he never gave anyone the impression that he was supernatural. His sanctity exhibited itself not only in the unity of his religious life, his teaching and his pastoral preaching, but in his devotion at prayer. He often wept when saying Mass or during the singing of the lovely chant, *Media Vita* ("In the midst of life, we are in death; do not abandon us, Lord.") He would be so concentrated in thought that he could be cut, without pain, by a doctor or shout out unexpectedly during a meal, legends says.

In 1256 he became a Master of Theology and between 1256 and 1264 he wrote the *Summa Theologiae* as a sort of introductory theology text for students. He became the pope's theologian in 1261 and preached in Rome and wherever the papal court moved. An outstanding and popular preacher, his sermons were simple, deep and balanced. After Pope Urban's death, he taught in Bologna, but was called back to serve Pope Clement IV as his theologian.

When he returned to Paris, he was a central figure in the debates between the seculars and regulars, between the more traditional theologians and those willing to use new sources. During a three-year period, he was asked to debate the question of truth 253 times. His health must have been affected by the burden of teaching and preaching, because when he was appointed professor at Naples, and so left Paris for the last time, he rode a donkey rather than walked as he had done in all his long journeys before.

At Naples, he finished part of the third section of the *Summa* but spent much more time in contemplation, never finishing the whole work. After December 6, 1272, he wrote no more. Legend says he made several attempts to burn the *Summa*; that he had a sense it was all so much straw. Some think that the vision of Christ which he had that December day caused his dismay with the distance between what he saw in Christ and what he was trying to say.

There is no doubt that he spent more and more time in prayer and that his health was bad. He took a leave of absence to regain his strength and visited his sister Theodora. Thomas was ordered to go to the Council of Lyons, but he never made it. Riding along abstracted in thought, he was injured by hitting a fallen tree. After receiving care from his niece for a while, he was taken to the Cistercian Abbey at Fossa Nuova where he was tenderly cared for by the monks as he lay dying for a month. Courteously he thanked them for their care and with great difficulty granted their request to comment on the *Canticle of Canticles*. Legend has it that he stopped at the line, "Come my beloved, let us go forth into the fields." Receiving viaticum before the assembled community, he recited the *Adoro Te* and died the next day, March 7, 1274.

Thomas is not a "flashy" saint — his holiness reminds me of what Hopkins said of another quiet man:

> Honor is flashed off exploit, so we say;
> And those strokes once that gashed flesh or galled
> shield Should tongue that time now,
> trumpet now that field,
> And, on the fight, forge his glorious day.
> On Christ they do and on the martyr may
> But be the war within, the brand we wield
> Unseen, the heroic break not outward steeled,
> Earth hears no hurtle then from fiercest fray.
> Yet God (that hews mountain and continent,
> Earth, all, out; who, with trickling increment,
> Veins violets and tall trees makes more and more)
> Could crowd career with conquest while there went
> Those years and years by of world without event
> That in Majorca Alfonso watched the door.
> ("St. Alphonsus Rodriguez" from Gerard Manley Hopkins,
> *Poems and Prose* [NY: Penguin Books, 1980])

Thomas is a sturdy rock of patience, building by increment, attentive to detail — let his mother rage, his brothers fight, he would channel his passions into deeper, steadier, larger places. These are passions of the mind; no wonder his work was so enduring. Thomas had endurance and patience and steadiness. He was the long distance runner, the marathon-winner who does not run in quick bursts yet still wins.

His sobriety and silence are not chilling, however; he was a man of too deep friendships to have no heart. Certain passages in the *Summa* are warm and comforting in their common sense. How to alleviate sorrow? Thomas answers: "Good sleep, a bath and a glass of wine." Thomas says that if a person wants to weep, the best thing to do is to let him weep. Do you want to get the most out of life? Thomas advises work, because he says fun is a relaxation from work and a preparation for work. "Without work it is impossible to have fun," he concludes — surely with a glint in his eye, as he must have had, too, when he wrote: "The most hopeful people in the world are the young and the drunk. The first because they have little experience with failure, and the second because they have succeeded in drowning theirs."

> *Brother Thomas, Prince of Theologians, so long kept at a distance by those who use you as a "commecial" for what they want to sell, help me to keep faith in uniting theology and spirituality; let me not use you as a "commercial" for my notions; help me be happy, to be hidden, not seeking to be thought special; help me think passionately and clearly. Gentle helper, lover of truth, stubborn against intrusion — lend me your gentleness and truthful stubbornness.*

FOR PERSONAL REFLECTION

1. What aspect of St. Thomas' personality attracts you the most?
2. Do you find it hard to see how great learning and great faith can go together?   Do you see how St. Thomas is an example of how this can be done?

3. Some people thought St. Thomas was stupid because he did not talk much.   Think of a time when you underestimated someone you know.

4. What do you think of St. Thomas' remedies for sorrow?   Do they fit in with your own ideas of spirituality?

ST. CATHERINE of SIENA (1347-1380)

Ronda Chervin

The story of St. Catherine of Siena, although less well known than that of St. Francis of Assisi, is as spectacular, colorful and endearing.

Who would not be amazed to read about a woman proclaimed a Doctor of the Church who was illiterate until taught to read by Jesus Himself?

Who would expect a contemplative visionary to flourish, not in a convent or even on a mountain top, but in the role of cook and maid in her own huge family of which she was the 24th child? Who would think that one through whom sublime theological doctrine flowed so that it required sometimes five priestly scribes to take down the thoughts she receive in locutions, would be willing to spend the rest of her day tending those so ill and cantankerous that no one would nurse them? How exciting to ponder the life of one so ascetic that she neither ate nor drank for the last years of her life, who was yet affectionately known as Mama to her hundreds of disciples.

These facts and others like them can be found in the *Life of St. Catherine of Siena*, by Blessed Raymond of Capua. It should be noted that Raymond, sure that many would find the miracles of Catherine hard to believe, devotes many pages to proving his own credentials as a theologian, spiritual director, and Dominican, to show that he was a worthy discerner of spirits. Blessed Raymond was the disciple of Catherine as well as her spiritual director and confessor, and his account is much more vivid and personal than any of the modern historical biographies. In fact, I found that I could not enjoy Catherine's own book, *The Dialogue*, until I had read Raymond's tale of her life, so much does he illumine the nature of this saint's witness.

To summarize briefly St. Catherine's life:

Born in 1347 to a devout working class family of dyers, the Benincasas, Catherine came into the world as a twin — the 24th child of her robust mother. Her twin sister died very shortly after birth, causing such consternation that the couple quickly managed to produce another baby as a replacement. Myself a twin, and mother of identical twins, I have often pondered the psychological and spiritual legacy of such a unique experience. Not only leaving the closeness to the mother of the womb, which all babies have to suffer, a twin is also separated from the little one he/she lived right next to since conception. I speculate that many twins spend their lives trying to recapture that unity, and if religiously inclined, may have a definite psychosomatic edge in the knowledge of and longing for identity with God. Other saints who were twins are Thomas the Apostle, Thomas Aquinas, Benedict and Scholastica. In the case of Catherine, one could describe her relationship to Christ as one of twinliness, so intensely did she long to duplicate Him in her own flesh.

In our day when people consider that one or two children is about enough, it is rather thrilling to me to consider that one of the most powerful and influential women in Church history should have been the 24th child. It says to me that extreme generosity in child-bearing is somehow related to extreme richness of spirit. The daughter of such life-loving parents would spend herself to bring divine life to even one single soul.

The little Catherine was, from earliest childhood, so charming and wise, though never especially pretty, that relatives and neighbors vied for the opportunity to take her into their homes. At the age of six she was gifted with a miraculous grace powerful enough to shape the rest of her life.

Running an errand with her older brother, she paused to glance across the valley. "There in the sky above the roof of the church of the Friars Preachers (the Dominicans), she saw the vision of a splendid audience-hall, furnished like a royal court. Within it was the Savior of the world . . . with him were Peter and Paul and John the Evangelist. Entranced and rooted to the spot, she fixed her eyes on the sight . . . (He) smiled on her with surpassing affection, stretched out his hand over her and made the Sign of the Cross . . . she was transported out of herself . . . she lost all consciousness . . . Stefano (her brother) called out to her two or three times to attract her attention . . . like a person awaking from a heavy sleep she . . . said 'Oh, if you but saw what I am looking at, you would never try to take me away from a sight so delightful.' " (Blessed Raymond of Capua, pp. 29-30)

This vision, which reminds us of those experienced in our century by children seeing apparitions of Mary, caused great changes in the young girl. She began to withdraw from the family to be alone in prayer. She was seen to levitate off the ground. When she was seven years old she made a vow of consecration to Christ hoping to be His bride. She gradually began to fast more and more.

Not given much to supernatural visions, it is hard for me to imagine a child having such an experience. Yet my whole life was changed by the few exterior visions (as opposed to interior visions seen within) that I had when still a non-believer. Once, I saw the face of Christ in a painting come alive, and the face of Pope Pius XII assume the same luminous expression as that of Christ in the painting. Years later, I saw my twin-sister's face become that of Christ. The first two visions made me a believer in the divinity of Christ and in the holiness to be found in the Church. The second was accompanied by receiving the charismatic gifts of the Spirit. When I recount such moments to other believers, I find that at least half of them have had some peak experience of a similar sort. So, "miracles" are not that rare even in our skeptical times. My feeling is that some personality types are more open to the supernatural than others. One saint remarked that those who do not have ecstasies in prayer often have more in life. This may also be the case. Others may be called for the journey of pure faith, to be rewarded still more richly in eternity without any veils at all.

To return to the story of Catherine, the Benincasa parents were not overjoyed at the pious behavior of their beloved daughter. They had been dreaming of the good match they could make for her once she turned twelve, the usual time for engagements. When they tried to persuade her to adorn herself to look attractive, she refused. Finally, they brought her to her married sister who convinced her to agree to conform outwardly even while stubbornly vowing that she would never marry anyone, but remain a virgin for the Lord. Later, Catherine was to view this acquiescence as a terrible sin. What had induced her to give in? Was it not preferring her sister to Christ Himself?

Such concern may strike us as ridiculously scrupulous. Those who study the saints claim, however, that the sense of sin is greatly magnified by the closeness to Christ. An analogy which might help is this: an infidelity in marriage on the part of a woman married to a truly saintly husband would seem to us and to her as much more grave than the same infidelity on the part of a woman married to a cruel wife-beater. Think of the scourging remorse of Tolstoy's Natasha in *War and Peace* for her betrayal of so good a accent is too high fiancé. Catherine's parents tried to introduce her to potential husbands. Their daughter would flee from the room. Desperate, they brought her to a Dominican confessor in the hope that he would insist that she obey her parents. Instead, he became convinced that she had a special vocation and advised her to chop off her long hair as a sign of her steadfastness.

Such acts infuriated her parents to such an extent that they decided to punish her by exiling her from the little closet-like cell she liked to retire to, and making her serve as cook and maid to the whole family. They thought this might show her that it would be better to be married to a rich man than to persist in her rebellion.

Undaunted, Catherine decided that she should make a secret cell in her heart talking all day long with her beloved God while outwardly doing her chores. Joyfully singing hymns to the Lord, she fulfilled all her duties without a word of complaint.

One day her father, seeing a holy dove above her head, decided he had been wrong. He assembled the family whom he had instructed to insult Catherine and told them, "We can never make a match for her which can be compared to this. We need not think we are the losers if we receive into our home not a mortal man, but him who is immortal, God and man." (Blessed Raymond of Capua, p. 52)

What a fascinating combination of assertiveness and passivity, we might remark! Catherine insisted on getting her way, not because it was her way, but because she was convinced it was what God wanted. Yet she didn't scream and yell at her parents' insensitivity to her vocation. Instead she obeyed, and in so doing won them over.

One of the most amazing graces given to Catherine was her gradual ability to fast, finally leading to not eating at all. By her twentieth year Catherine ate only cooked vegetables. For the last decade of her life she took no food at all and slept only a half-hour every couple of days. Yet she had great energy, more so than many of her male followers. Doubters should investigate documented cases by scientists of present-day stigmatists who took no food for many years.

How can we relate ourselves to such unusual facts? I, who tend to require food every two hours, nonetheless in times of great concentration on some task, such as writing a book, or occasionally when my prayer has been exceptionally deep, find that I am less famished. "Man does not live by bread alone." Many people with diet problems find that emotional healing leads to less ravenous an appetite. Some theologians speculate that in heaven food and drink will be taken only for celebration, since we will receive our energy directly from God.

Some people are alienated by accounts of miracles; but most of us, I think, find the doubting Thomas in us bows down in the face of clear evidence of the supernatural and says, "My Lord and my God."

For those who insist on deeds of love rather than miracles (indeed one main criteria for canonization — heroic charity), our Sienese saint is ready to dazzle you as well. Listen to this description by Blessed Raymond:

"On one occasion, when she (Catherine) happened to be so ill that her whole body was swollen up from head to foot and she could not get out of bed or put a foot under her, she heard of a poor widow who lived in the district adjoining her own. This poor woman had a family of boys and girls, all of them suffering great hunger and want. Catherine's heart was moved with compassion, and when night came on she prayed her Lord to give her back for the time being strength enough to bring help to the poor woman. And there and then, before dawn broke, she got up and began to ransack the house. She got a sack and filled it with wheaten meal, a great glass bottle which she filled with wine, another bottle which she filled with oil and such eatables as she could find, bringing them all to her little cell. But it was one thing to be able to bring these articles one by one to her cell, and quite another to find the strength to carry them all together the whole way to the widow's house. It seemed impossible. However, she took up the goods and fastened them about her weak body, one article on her right arm, another on her left, something on her shoulders, something else hanging from her waist. Then, placing her hope in the help of heaven, she made an effort to stand upright laden with her burden. Instantly, by God's wonderful help, she heaved it all up with such ease that it felt as if each of the things she carried had been drained completely of its weight. . . . And yet, according to a careful reckoning which I (Raymond) worked out myself, the goods which she was carrying at the time would normally have weighed about a hundred pounds." (Blessed Raymond of Capua, p. 147)

Such stories are typical of Catherine, for her charity toward the needy knew no bounds. I cannot recount all of the stories documented by Blessed Raymond, but urge instead that you read his book.

What inspires me so much is that someone with such marked contemplative gifts would be willing to concern herself about such matters. Surely she could have excused herself on the grounds that there were others in the Church who could deliver food or nurse the sick, whereas she had been chosen for transmitting extraordinary revelations. I would certainly take such a stance if it were I. But perhaps not.

History shows that it is a mark of all the saints to go out of their way to help the needy. Being drawn so close to God, and responding with all their hearts, such men and women no longer focus on or worry about themselves. Instead of their spare time being filled with works required to take care of themselves, they leave all this in the hands of God and then find themselves free to aid others.

In fact, that is my own experience. When I am very close to Christ in prayer, the tasks I had set for myself in the house or at the University can be accomplished at twice the speed. At times when I have awakened in the night with illuminations, I feel so rested from immersion in the life of the Prince of Peace that I am not half as tired as on nights when I go to sleep full of anxieties, sleep for eight hours, and still arise fatigued. As Raymond frequently remarks (sometimes to shame his apparently lax Dominican brethren), all this time Catherine was living for Christ without guidance from a community, without the help of living examples, solely moved by the Spirit.

But Catherine longed to be part of an order, and had always been drawn to the Dominicans.

Her mother, who was overly fond of her, refused to let her join such an order. However, there was a third order of widows who took vows but lived in their homes, attending Mass frequently and visiting the poor and the sick. They wore a habit which is described by Raymond in this way:

"It was a habit of white and black which our Fathers designed to be worn as a symbol of innocence and of humility, the white symbolizing innocence and the black humility. . . . (It) aptly represented the habit of soul of this holy maid. In her outward life she was making every effort to mortify — to put to death whatever of unregenerate, fallen nature still lived in her, with its death-dealing pride; and this was aptly signified by black. In her inward life, in soul as well as in body, she had made virginal purity her ideal, that by it she might draw near with all her powers to her eternal Spouse and share the brightness of him who is the true Light itself; and this was no less aptly signified by white." (Blessed Raymond of Capua, p. 68)

The richness of the color symbolism is one of the reasons why priests, sisters, and religious brothers used to all wear special garb. Many younger novices, in orders which have dropped the habit to stress their oneness with all humankind, ask to retain at least some part of it. They seem to sense the need to express the inward in outer forms.

As a woman living in the world, in a family and professional setting, I still find clothing to be quite symbolic. I tend to wear drab, formal clothing when I feel insecure at work and think to prove that I fit in by dressing conservatively. When happy, I want to wear bright ethnic clothing.

Having come to a new level of union with God in prayer, I found myself buying more and more white blouses and dresses — as if revelling in my new-found purity of heart.

Catherine wanted to join this Third Order of Dominicans; however, her mother tried everything to dissuade her, still hoping that her strange but beloved daughter would snap out of it and get married. The women in the group, not having met her, feared that a girl so young might bring shame to them by breaking the vows.

Providence intervened in a most amusing way. Catherine developed a terrible case of acne. When delegates from the Order came to see her, she looked so dreadful that they decided she would not be a coquette. Most importantly, they were won by the depth of her commitment to Christ and the Church.

After this, she began a long period of silent contemplation. Catherine spent all her time in her room, leaving only for Church. Christ spoke to her both inwardly and sometimes by making Himself visible, even walking up and down with her while she prayed. Raymond relates with his own characteristic charm:

"Our Lord himself became her frequent visitor; and to such a degree that it would be hard to find two people who spent their time so constantly in each other's company as these two did: this holy maiden and her Spouse, the Savior of mankind. Even when she was speaking to others this divine Vision would sometimes stand beside her, and while her tongue was speaking to her fellow-men her inner self was taken up in converse with him. But such a state of tension between the visible and the Invisible never lasted long. The attraction of her Spouse would irresistibly assert itself, and in a moment or two she would become abstracted from her senses and fall into ecstasy." (Raymond of Capua, pp. 78-79)

There are some readers who may seriously doubt that all this can be true. Accustomed to a life of faith-in-darkness, the idea of anyone living in the felt-supernatural presence of God day by day seems incredible.

After reading many lives of the saints, I have come to several conclusions about such experiences.

There seems to be little relationship between visions and virtue at the outset. Some mystics are innocent and fervent from birth, but many were great sinners whose lives changed dramatically because of special graces from God. Many highly virtuous people are not mystics at all. The mystics themselves often asked God why they, frail, weak creatures that they were, should receive such gifts and others more holy receive few or none.

The answer seems always to involve the mystery of God's love. Those who can be good without visions are lauded for their humble perseverance. Those gifted are often told that it is because of their weakness that they need such unusual encouragement. As St. Paul, a great sinner turned saint, wrote, "I glory in my weaknesses" (2 Cor 12:5). "The weak things of the world I have chosen" (1 Cor 1:27). The conclusion I draw from observation of contemporaries is that there are two main characteristics which favor reception of mystical gifts: an extreme yearning for love, or a sublime purity of heart.

The longing for affirmation may be caused either by psychological deprivation in childhood, or paradoxically by its opposite. Some people fall into a dull resignation because they rarely received the love they wanted. These do not usually become contemplatives, for they are reasonably content to be free of great pain, and tend to hide their emotional needs beneath a show of stoicism. But others refuse to give up. They are willing to be vulnerable and open to new wounds if only there is some hope of finally getting the love they crave.

If such a person turns to God for help, he or she may often be the one to experience God's love in a vivid manner. If sensitivity is also linked to an imaginative bent, the visions may be exterior as well as interior.

On the other hand, some of the mystics of the past and present are persons who enjoyed deep love in childhood, and being shocked by the coldness of the outside world, seek to find it in God.

However, from time to time I meet a religious person with no such psychological history — someone so "normal" in temperament and character that one would hardly notice him/her in any group of people. Of these, the mystic ones are those with an astounding purity of heart. They are individuals who early or late in life, simply realize that God alone is the source of all truth, goodness, life, beauty and happiness, and decide to devote themselves without stint to loving God and neighbor as themselves. Because they have no other goal than love, there is nothing to stand between them and the presence of God.

If you happen to be someone who longs to be closer to God, but cannot seem to figure out how, the saints advise you not to be envious of mystics. All those who follow Christ will experience Him directly in the Kingdom for all eternity. Those who have visions of Him now also have terrible trials, so dreadful that you might not want to exchange places with them for anything in the world.

As vividly as Catherine experienced God, so intimately did she come in contact with demons. They would come to her and torture her with evil thoughts, throw her into the fireplace, from which God would save her miraculously, assault her with despairing thoughts so that she would doubt everything Christ had told her in His locutions.

"Poor creature, what do you intend to do? Will you spend your whole life in this state of misery? For, unless you yield to us, we will never slacken our assaults on you until the day you die," the devils would say.

To which Catherine replied with amazing courage: "I have

made choice of suffering as the well-spring of my strength. It is no hardship for me, but rather a delight, to endure for my Savior's name all you have been inflicting on me, and more besides, for as long as it shall please his Majesty." At these words, Raymond relates, "the demon horde turned tail and fled pell-mell, and a great light from heaven flooded the little room. And there, at the heart of the brightness, was our Lord Jesus Christ, himself nailed upon the cross and covered with his blood . . . from that cross he spoke to her these words: 'My daughter Catherine, look at what I have suffered for your sake. Do not take it hard, then, when you too must suffer something for my sake.' " (Blessed Raymond of Capua, p. 101)

In my preface to this book, I mentioned that I admired the saints so much for their logic. See how Catherine outwits the Devil himself simply by the strength of her perfect faith. And we, so often, with our anemic theology, do not have the supernatural logic of faith with which to meet our temptations. Resting too much on human reason and the humanitarian forms of ethics, we imagine that we can be good on our own. Then, when the hour of temptation comes, we are caught by the Devil's lies. Weakened by self-indulgence, we cannot bear to imagine that sacrifice might be called for, sacrifice beyond our own strength. But we do not believe enough in the Lord to think that He could suddenly remove these demons — demons of alcohol, depression, burnout, disordered sex, gluttony, or resentment. And so believing neither in Satan nor in the power of God, we are slowly but surely defeated as we move gradually, oh so gradually, from naive idealism to bitter cynicism.

But not Catherine. Against the Devil, Christ always wins. She had committed herself totally to Him, and in that belief she would live, even if He took away all her visions and left her a victim for her whole life on earth.

Note, also, that there is nothing detached about our Italian saint. The intensity of John of the Cross led him to a transcendent peace through detachment. His love for Christ has a lyrical, poetic character. But the intensity of Catherine is a burning fire of identification with the Crucified One, and also burning joy in His triumphs.

The words she speaks to Christ and He to her are as fiery as those of any lovers in an Italian opera — and as full of blood and death. Her deep life in God insured, however, that the end of her "opera" was not tragedy but a burst of glory.

Let us listen in on some of the words between God and Catherine from the *Dialogue* which she dictated to her priestly scribes:

About the last degree of union of the soul and God, Catherine hears God: ". . . they are enflamed and submerged in the blood, where they find my burning charity. This charity is a fire that comes forth from me and carries off their heart and spirit, accepting the sacrifice of their desires. Then their mind's eye rises up and gazes into my Godhead, and love follows understanding to be nourished there and brought into the union. This is a vision through infused grace that I give to the soul who loves and serves me in truth." (St. Catherine, p. 155)

"True, the people of the world do not offer me (God) glory in the way they ought, by loving me above all things. But my mercy and my charity are reflected in them because I lend them time and do not order the earth to swallow them up for their sins. No, I look on them and order the earth to give them a share of its fruits." (St. Catherine, p. 150)

Catherine, trying to win mercy for a dying woman who was persecuting her, begs God to change this woman's heart and convert her.

"My Lord, is it for this purpose that my miserable self was brought into the world: that by occasion of me, souls created in your own image should be condemned to everlasting fire? Can it possibly be your will to permit that I, who am in duty bound to help my sister to eternal salvation, should instead become to her

the occasion of everlasting damnation? Far be such a fearful
sentence from your immeasurable mercy! Far be it from your
eternal goodness to permit a thing so dreadful. . . . Is this how
you keep those gracious promises you made me when you said
that my life would bear fruit in the salvation of the souls of my
neighbors? . . . I will never give over pleading with your infinite
goodness until . . . my sister has been saved from everlasting
death." (St. Catherine, p. 143)

Apparently, God replied that His justice could not permit
such obstinate and deliberate hatred to remain unpunished.
Catherine replied, "My Lord, never while life is in me will I
move a foot from this place until you grant me for my sister the
mercy I have asked. Make me pay the penalty for any sin of
hers. . . ." (St. Catherine, p. 144) The dying woman struggled in
her death agony but could not die until finally God sent a radiant
light to her, and she confessed her sins and asked Catherine for
forgiveness.

"After her death the Lord granted Catherine a vision of
that soul, now saved. Its beauty was so great, that no words could
describe its loveliness . . . 'would not anyone endure the greatest
trials in order to win so exquisite a creature? I myself am Beauty
Supreme from which all other beauty is derived. Yet so enchant-
ing is the beauty of the souls of men that I gladly came down
upon this earth and shed my Blood in order to redeem them.' "
(St. Catherine, p. 144)

These quotations came from a later part of Catherine's life.
For after the time of staying in her cell and praying night and
day, also doing harsh penance, wearing heavy chains on her
body and sleeping on hard boards, the Lord one day told her she
must leave her cell and go back into the world, to speak to others
of Him and serve Him in the Church. She protested that it would
be a great anguish to leave the intimacy of her hidden life and
that no one would listen to her anyhow since she was an
uneducated woman.

The answer the Lord gave her sounds delightful in the ears of Christian feminists. He said that He wanted to humble the pride of the learned theologians who lacked Catherine's fire, by sending a woman to evangelize them.

Catherine certainly was called to evangelize weaker brethren. The book she dictated called *The Dialogue* was the result of locution given her in trance. The theology in them is so authoritative and masculine in tone that it is almost impossible to imagine that they came from the lips of an uneducated woman. They have none of the sweet, pious tone of most feminine writings on spirituality.

Let me quote a few more examples:

"Do you know, daughter, who you are and who I am? If you know these two things you have beatitude in your grasp. You are she who is not, and I AM WHO IS. Let your soul but become penetrated with this truth, and the Enemy can never lead you astray; you will never be caught in any snare of his, nor ever transgress any commandment of mine; you will have set your feet on the royal road which leads to the fulness of grace, and truth, and light." (Blessed Raymond of Capua, p. 83)

"Your mercy made Your Son play death against life and life against death on the wood of the Cross. . . . 'As much as you long to see Me honored in holy Church, just so much must you conceive the love it takes to suffer willingly and with true patience.'" (St. Catherine, p. 58)

(Those in union with God when aware of the sins of others) "live in this gentle light . . . therefore they are always peaceful and calm, and nothing can scandalize them because they have done away with what causes them to take scandal, their self-will. . . . They find joy in everything. They do not sit in judgment on my servants or anyone else, but rejoice in every situation and every way of living they see, saying, 'Thanks to you, eternal Father, that in your house there are so many dwelling places.' And they are happier to see many different ways than if

they were to see everyone walking the same way, because this
way they see the greatness of my goodness more fully revealed . . . even when they see something that is clearly sinful
they do not pass judgment, but rather feel a holy and genuine
compassion, praying for the sinner. . . ." (St. Catherine, pp.
189-190)

In fact by the end of her life she had become a public figure,
journeying to Florence and Pisa and Rome and Avignon in-
structing Cardinals and Popes about the will of God.

This chapter will be too long if I go into more detail, but I
do not want to conclude without mentioning the great love she
had for Holy Communion. Some imagine that those who receive
direct communication with God in prayer would have no need
for "so-called" external rituals. In the case of most mystics,
however, including Catherine, the inner personal experience of
God made them all the more able to appreciate the significance
of His presence within the material symbols of the Church.

Given such singular graces as drinking from the open side
of the crucified Lord in a vision, Catherine yet hungered and
thirsted for the Eucharist. In fact, the Holy Body of Christ in the
Communion wafer was her only food. In those times daily
communion was rare. When she finally got permission to receive every day, she was still blocked, for after receiving the
divine Lord she would usually fall into a trance. Her body would
become so rigid that it was impossible to move her from the
spot, and this interfered with the practice of closing the Church
for the noontime siesta. Accordingly, she was forbidden to
receive every day. However, when Raymond became her confessor and companion she could have the Bread of Life whenever
he said his private Mass. When this was delayed by circumstances beyond their control, she would come to him and
whisper passionately, "I am dying of hunger, could you not say
Mass soon."

God told Catherine about the Eucharist.

"And what food is this? It is the body and blood of Christ crucified, wholly human, the food of angels and the food of life. It is a good that satisfies the hungry soul who finds joy in this bread, but not those who are not hungry, for it is a good that must be taken with the mouth of holy desire and tasted in love." (St. Catherine, p. 279)

Finally, Catherine was to receive the stigmata which were invisible except for a wound near the heart. She died in Rome at the age of 33 after many days of torment, again demons having come to battle one last time for the soul of this heroine of God. Many of her disciples surrounded her on her deathbed from which she gave many instructions and teachings.

"Then, when she saw her last hour had finally come, she said: 'Lord, into your hands I commend my spirit.' With these words that holy soul attained what she had yearned for so long: released from this mortal flesh she became one, in an inseparable and everlasting union, with that Spouse of hers whom she had loved with a love unutterable." (Blessed Raymond of Capua, p. 340)

Many miracles occurred after her death. My favorite concerns a woman of Rome who was in the habit of going on pilgrimage from church to church. On the day of Catherine's death this disciple was delayed in making lunch for her family, but she felt so drawn to the Mass that she left without putting the soup on the fire. In her absence Catherine came and cooked the soup for her, as was later revealed in a vision, thus ending her stay on earth again in the role of house-maid.

While reading Raymond's biography of Catherine, I found myself often infused with the same kind of fire she experienced. A great thirst for holiness would come over me, a burning desire for the Eucharist, and for the conversion of others, as well as a longing to be as she was, a slave to the needs of others.

But then between readings I would wonder how anyone

could imitate Catherine. Especially, how could so weak a person as myself, who can hardly stand to have my teeth cleaned or to endure a rainy day, think of being like this saint of asceticism? Does God really want us to suffer such torments?

And God Himself tells Catherine that He takes no pleasure in sufferings themselves, but only in the generosity of the one who accepts pain for love of Him. He also told her that not all are called to ascetical practices, for each is different in temperament and constitution.

Yet, one cannot read Catherine's *Life* or *Dialogue* without truly wondering if one is not called to do much, much more for the Kingdom. In a burst of enthusiasm I decided that in my circumstances the only way to follow Catherine was to become a slave to everyone — simply do everything anyone asked of me with sweet compliance and not a single complaint.

You would have to know me to imagine what a sacrifice this would be. Vastly over-extended as my energies are, I am bombarded with petty requests from members of the family wanting rides, cups of tea, help with pesky tasks. It has taken me years of prayer and counseling to develop the assertiveness to say no to unreasonable requests, instead of building up hostility and letting it out in temper tantrums.

I tried becoming a slave for a few days but became very depressed. Finally I called my spiritual director. He laughed. "God already has Catherine, now He wants you." He added that in my situation it would just make other people commit sins of laziness if I let them make me their slave. Instead, I should justly assert my own rights and needs, but then, be patient with others and as generous as I can be without driving myself crazy.

This advice was a great relief, yet it left me feeling at an impasse. How then should I be influenced by Catherine, if I could not be ascetical due to a weak physical constitution, and not be a slave without psychological trauma?

When I pray about it, what comes to me is that I should be

as faithful to God as Catherine was, in doing His will *for me*. When I believe as deeply, love as strongly, and give of myself as courageously as she did, always getting sustenance from the prayer of union, then I am . . . God's holy Ronda.

FOR PERSONAL REFLECTION

1. Describe times when you have felt the heavens open or seen visions, whether interior or exterior.   If you have never had such an experience, what would be your peak experiences of beauty, or truth, or love?   How have these shaped your life?
2. Does your family understand your spirituality?   If not, how have you experienced that rift?
3. Do you have a cell in your home or in your heart where you can be close to God?
4. Catherine's load of food for the poor grew lighter as she prayed.   When you take up a burden willingly for Christ for love of others do you find it less than you expected?
5. Which miracles described in Scripture or in lives of holy people have strengthened your faith most?
6. How does the color of your clothing reflect the values you hold dear?
7. How does the Devil tempt you?   Can you find victory in prayer?
8. Is there fire in your relationship to God?   His to you?
9. Do you think there is a difference between masculine and feminine spirituality?   If so, when do you find yourself exemplifying each of these?
10. Have you ever experienced hunger for Holy Communion? If not, have you ever prayed to discern Christ's presence more clearly?
11. What message did Catherine leave you with?

ST. JOAN of ARC (1412-1431)

Mary Neill

More has been written about this young woman, the Maid of Orleans who fought to liberate France from the English during the middle ages, than about any other saint. Writers and artists find fascinating the story of a young maiden who, because of a vision she saw at thirteen and of Voices she never ceased to hear until the day that she was burned at the stake at nineteen, blazed like a meteor of spiritual power into the men's world of war-games and inquisition courts only to be adoringly followed and rapidly killed.

Over 200 books have been written about her and several plays and films. She stands clearly revealed in the records of the long trial hearings that preceded her death. She submitted to fifteen interrogations in 25 days, tired and taunted by jailers. She leaps from the pages of the manuscript, startlingly, with a voice like no other — unlettered (she could sign only X for her name), wise, humorous, courageous (she refused the lawyer the court offered), humble, stubborn and utterly convinced that in obeying the inner Voices (which she saw as St. Michael or St. Catherine or St. Margaret) she was obeying God's will — the will of a God who was interested in interfering in politics. Her God was one who cared which man was the king of France; who cared whether France ceased to exist as a nation; who could use a teen-aged girl to turn the tide in the warfare because the girl believed and followed His will — not her own. Here are excerpts that reveal her voice:

> As far as my religious upbringing was concerned, I was well and truly brought up as a child should be. It was my mother who taught me to recite the Our Father, the Hail Mary and the Creed. It was she alone who taught me my faith.

It also was this mother who, twenty years after Joan's death, entered Notre Dame in Paris accompanied by a large group of prelates and laymen to make her claim for justice against her daughter's unjust trial.

Joan was not a rebellious child, acting out authority problems. Biddable to her family, she was biddable to God:

> I was in complete subjection to my father and mother and obeyed them implicitly until after my departure from home. They almost went out of their minds when I set forth for Vaucouleurs, but when I wrote them afterward, they forgave me.

To an inquisitor with a thick Limoges accent who asked her, "In what tongue do your Voices speak?", she replied, "In a better one than yours." As she mounted her horse while holding her banner emblazoned *Jesus Maria* she called to her soldiers, "Let all those who love me, follow me." When she was asked by pious people to touch their rosaries, she laughed and passed them to her hostess: "Touch them yourself; your touch will be as effective as mine."

Joan had a sharp eye and ear for distinguishing true from false voices. She followed the truth of love, not lies, so her men followed her.

> As for my jump from the dungeon at Beaurevoir, which I made against the command of my Voices, I could not restrain myself from the attempt. And when my Voices saw my compulsion and that I could not help myself, they came to my aid and saved me from killing myself. For two or three days after my fall, I was unwilling to take food. All that time St. Catherine comforted me, telling me to confess my sins and ask pardon from God for having made the jump.

Joan had no illusions about her frailty or the willingness of God to forgive and comfort her. When forbidden to leave the prison, she replied:

> I do not accept this prohibition. If ever I succeed in making my escape, no one can accuse me of breaking faith or going back on my word, for I have given no promise. Further I have to protest at being kept in chains and manacles. . . . It is true that I wished to escape and still do so, for every prisoner has the right to try to escape.

Her meekness was not cowardice. Her sense of faithfulness and justice was central. Her promise meant something. When they tried to question her femininity because she wore men's clothes, she boasted:

> Yes, I learned how to sew and spin linen; in the manner of sewing and spinning I can hold my own with any woman in Rouen.

Her inwardness was steady; her desire, the winning of the hardest battle:

There is not a day that I do not hear it (the Voice). I have never asked anything of my Voice save the salvation of my soul.

She boldly challenged her interrogators again and again:

By my Faith, there are certain things which, if you ask me, I shall not tell you. For example, I have sworn to tell nothing about the revelations made to me and if I now swear to do so, I shall be guilty of perjury. Be careful of what you do, for you are taking a heavy responsibility upon yourself and imposing too heavy a burden on me.

Interrogator: When you saw your Voices, was any special light visible?

    Joan: Light shines on others besides you.

When asked about her sword taken from the enemy, she replied: "I carried it at Compiegne because it was a fine weapon, capable of dealing shrewd blows."

The trial proceedings testify to the shrewd verbal blows Joan could make. She had a deadly inner certainty in the face of injustice. When Joan testified that her Voice was beautiful, gentle and humble and spoke the French language, the inquisitor demanded: "Why did not St. Margaret speak in English?" Joan replied: "Why should she speak English, since she does not support the English cause?" (Article I:10 of her condemnation by the court would declare that it was "contrary to the precept of charity" to state that Ss. Catherine and Margaret did not speak English.)

Interrogator: Do you possess any rings?

    Joan: You took one from me; give it back to me.

Interrogator: Did St. Michael appear to you naked?

Joan: Think you that my Master had not wherewith to clothe him?

Interrogator: Would you agree to wear female attire in order to be permitted to attend mass?

Joan: I will ask counsel from on high and will answer that question later.

Interrogator: Do you submit to the judgment of the Church?

Joan: I submit to Our Lord, who sent me on my mission; to Our Lady, to all the blessed saints and the holy ones of paradise.

Interrogator: Then you do not submit to the Church?

Joan: As I see it, Our Lord and His Church are one, so there will be no difficulty there.

Interrogator: Would you feel bound to reveal the whole truth to the Pope?

Joan: I demand to be taken to him and I will give my answer before him.

When her inquisitors escalated their pressure and showed her a display of the instruments of torture ready to be used, Joan stood firm and said:

> Truly, should you tear me limb from limb and cause my soul to leave its body, I would tell you nothing but what I have already told. I have asked guidance from my Voices as to whether I should submit to the Church, and they have said to me: "If you wish your Master to come to your aid, you must leave the judgment of your actions to Him." I also asked my Voices if I would be burned, and in reply they told me: "Leave that in God's hands. He will help you."

At one point in the trial, pressured and confused, she signed a "cedula of abjuration" and put on women's attire. When she realized what she had done, through fear of fire, she resumed men's clothes and waited for the end:

> God sent word to me by St. Catherine and St. Margaret of the great pain to Him in the treason to which I consented in making abjuration and recantation in order to save my life. I did not know what was in the cedula of abjuration; I did not understand it at all.

When told she would be burned on the morning of May 30, she cried:

> Alas that I should be treated so horribly and cruelly that my entire body, which has never known impurity, should today be consumed and reduced to ashes. I would rather be decapitated seven times over than be thus burned. Before God, the great judge, I appeal against the great wrongs and injustices done to me. (She had had, earlier, to submit to physical examination to prove her virginity since it was considered that the Devil could not be working through a virgin.)

Joan's courage before her inquisitors, her slyness, her boldness combined with her transparency, and her vulnerability are a remarkable testimonial to an extraordinary Voice and grace. Whatever the nature of her Voices within may have been, her voice before the world — a hostile world — is unparalleled. She challenged her judges to be just; she begged mercy; but she never abandoned her inner conviction. And when she faltered, she moved back rapidly to her own center, guided lovingly by her Voices. (If only our inner voices were so lovely.) It was not in Churchmen's power to declare her God's good servant or not; her own conscience did that. Whatever her fear and trembling, she could not deny her inner truth.

All that was left for her was to die, and so she did, with shaven head and a paper mitre bearing the inscription, "Heretic, relapsed sinner, apostate, idolator." She protested, "I am neither heretic nor schismatic." She requested that a cross be held up to her. Unceasingly she called, "Jesus, St. Catherine, St. Michael." After the flames began crackling, she asked the priest holding the cross to step down, fearing for his safety. She begged for holy water, and when the fire roared all around her, through the smoke and flame she cried out loudly, "Jesus." Six times, "Jesus, Jesus, Jesus, Jesus, Jesus, Jesus." Then she died. When the fire was later quenched to prove to the still onlooking crowd that the Maid had been burned, her heart and other organs were intact in the ashes. They were thrown in the Seine. The crowd had been stunned by the way she died. The executioner kept repeating, "We have burned a saint." (The Churchmen who condemned her had left early in order to avoid ecclesiastical censure for watching an execution. Several of them were close to tears.)

Even as I write this account, I find it hard not to cry. How is such courage possible, such humanity, such gentleness, such faith in the midst of a world of war-games, word-games ("cedula of abjuration"), clothes-games, church-games? How does Christ in Joan of Arc ever break through the encrustation of "seeming" games in order to illumine *pure* being? Why is the price of living from *being*, rather than *seeming*, so great? Joan thought it ought to matter who was true king or not — it was no game to her. War was no game. She loved her soldiers and fought hard — taking her wounds without whining. She longed to hear Mass — it was no ritual game. Her inner truth was to be obeyed — it was no game. "Did St. Michael have hair?" they asked. "Why wouldn't he?" she replies. They condescend to her as hearing unreal voices, strange and exotic and dangerous, all the while ignoring the truth flowing from her voice, her face, her being, her deeds. They must kill this girl who says God crashed into her life, changing her history, her direction, her role, giving her power to storm castles, to speak the truth before kings and princes, to elicit love and respect from hard soldiers. They cannot bear to have this bold and sassy peasant show a king a power they knew not of. They will show her what power is: the power to kill, to bait, to destroy — to say, 500 years later, "Well, we made a mistake."

I feel such enormous passion and pain as I read the trial and death of Joan that I know it is related to games I've played in my life, games I've been caught in. But centrally, my passion for Joan ponders the generosity demanded by God, by life, by Christ in order to live from authentic being, to have an authentic voice, to follow your inner voice. The philosopher Martin Buber says, "One pays dearly for a life lived from being, but the price is never too dear." My body and soul protest as I read Joan's story. Sometimes the price seems too dear. It seems to me too dear as an onlooker. But if Joan, who never lied, said that God would be with her in that great final payment, I trust that He was — no, I trust her trust of Him. She knew Him well because she obeyed Him and was comforted by Him and His friends. "There is no bargain basement grace, no cheap grace," writes Bonhoeffer. No indeed.

Why don't more of us become friends of God, become saints, receive His crown and His comfort? To do so is to endanger our power in the world's games (the games grow tiresome, but we know them well) and we are addicted to looking good and feeling good rather than to *being* good. A woman rebuked me one morning after a lecture on this topic, saying, "I think you can both look good and be good." "Always?" I asked. "Well, yes." I think to myself, "Well, good luck, lady!" Later, as I write now about Joan, I also think:

Lady, when we do this, when we believe that the cross is not the way of Christ, we are the crowd that kills Joan of Arc, the mothers that abort being — not just in physical wombs, but wherever life appears gentle, vulnerable, strange, bold and challenging. This being is feminine, receptive, intuitive, circling, yielding, and needs the protection of the masculine; it needs to wear men's clothes, not to be raped, as Joan wore men's clothes to save her body in the prison.

The being wins, like Christ, by losing, by being overcome and being vindicated after death. I am convinced that when we pray, "Thy Kingdom Come", we assent that this mutilation of being, this killing of the Christ being in Joan of Arc and in every oppressed person is not God's will and that, as Christians, we must enter into His Kingdom so that such injustices be as uncommon on earth as they are in heaven. "No more war, no more, I say no more," Pope Paul VI pleaded at the United Nations. I add, "No more Joan of Arcs. No more."

St. Joan, if only I had been there at the trial (but they wouldn't have let me in, a woman) or had I been there to see you climbing the walls, or hearing Mass, or had I been brave enough to cry from the crowd, "Yes, Yes," when you said you were a loyal child of God. Do you hear me now, beyond time? My heart moves out to you over the years, and I feel the courage and love you had, pour into me. Help me see and help all the Joans, the Christs oppressed today. Let me trust and follow the Voice within me that says, No more — no more Joan of Arcs today. Being must be honored, the Voices within coloring the voices without. You died, not for nationalism, but for being. Our living to our deepest being, our deepest Voice will help us fight the nationalism that threatens to kill all living beings.

FOR PERSONAL REFLECTION

1. What is the quotation of Joan's that moves you the most?
2. When have you had an inner voice that you obeyed?

3. When have you considered the strange and exotic and dangerous?
4. Do you feel that Christ's crucifixion and Joan's burning are inevitable — that they will recur until the end of time? Is that the meaning of the cross?
5. What games do you play? When have you ever experienced their immense destruction?
6. How do you understand Joan's nationalism as relevant or irrelevant to today's world?

ST. THOMAS MORE (1478-1535)

Mary Neill

Few saints seem as accessible to our modern consciousness as
Thomas More who leaps across the four hundred years separat-
ing his time and ours to send a shudder of recognition and awe
into us who turn to his life for sustenance. For if Jesus is the
Bread of Life Who calls us to break open our lives, feed upon His
being and then freely feed others with ours, His saints have the
capacity to nourish us if we let them. Nowhere do I feel this
"Communion of Saints" so clearly as when I relish the bread of
St. Thomas More, who led a rich and abundant life. Of him
Robert Bolt writes:

> He parted with more than most men when he parted with his
> life, for he accepted and enjoyed his social context. (Introd. to
> *A Man for All Seasons*, p. xii)

"Indecently successful" as scholar, lawyer, ambassador, writer
and Lord Chancellor, he led an abundant life which he clung to
as carefully and wittily as he could until the clinging to it would
destroy his integrity, his self which was his God relationship.
(Bolt has him say to his friend Norfolk, "Affection goes as deep

in me as you think, but only God is love right through, Howard; and *that's* my *self.*")

He was a busy lover who adored and was adored by his large family and multiple friends. Of him his friend Erasmus, the most influential thinker of the time says:

> He seems to be born and made for friendship, of which he is the sincerest and most persistent devotee. Neither is he afraid of that multiplicity of friends of which Hesiod disapproves. Accessible to everyone, tender of intimacy, he is by no means fastidious in choosing his acquaintances. (*St. Thomas More,* John Farrow, p. 33)

Erasmus further speaks of his kindness and sweetness, his love of jokes, his lack of bitterness, his collection of birds, monkeys, foxes, ferrets and weasels he delighted in at his home in Chelsea. There, too, he kept any strange and curious objects he came across in his many travels as ambassador. He took double delight in the curiosity these aroused in visitors. Of his house (where even the king would come to talk in the garden with Thomas) Erasmus wrote:

> His house seems to have a sort of fatal felicity, no one having livd in it without being advanced to a higher fortune.

John Colet, another of More's illustrious friends, said of him that though England had many men of high intelligence, it had only one genius — More. Samuel Johnson wrote of him:

> He was the person of the greatest virtue these islands ever produced.

These social, intellectual, material and moral riches were crowned by a rich and deep piety. Erasmus says:

However averse he may be from all superstition, he is a steady adherent of true piety; having regular hours for his prayers, which are not uttered by rote, but from the heart. He talks with his friends about a future life in such a way as to make you feel that he believes what he says. . . . Such is More, even at court. *Even at court.* (Farrow, p. 33)

More's face was not a series of masks which he created to please whichever social context he was in. He trusted, loved, honored society; walked easily in it — but took his core identity, his empowerment, not from the social self, but the self hidden in God — and this, not without pain, but graciously, lightly — with fatal felicity.

Fatal felicity, too, accurately describes his farewell letter to his favorite daughter, Meg:

Farewell, my dear child, and pray for me and I shall for you and all your friends, that we may merrily meet in heaven.

Fatal felicity, too, his last pleasantry to the executioner not to strike till he had shifted his beard for that had never offended the king. More had, finally, a wonderful sense of his own self — this elusive self so searched for in our times.

Robert Bolt writes that More was:

. . . a man with an adamantine sense of his own self. He knew where he began and left off, what area of himself he could yield to the encroachments of his enemies, and what to the encroachments of those he loved. It was a substantial area in both cases, for he had a proper sense of fear and was a busy lover. Since he was a clever man and a great lawyer, he was able to retire from those areas in wonderfully good order, but at length he was asked to retreat from that final area where he located his self. And there this supple, humorous, unassum-

ing and sophisticated person set like metal, was overtaken by
an absolutely primitive rigor, and could no more be budged
than a cliff. (Bolt, p. xi)

What wonderful praise. He knew where he began and
where he left off. He did not hold himself back from the
encroachments of his love and work; he gave generously (where
one might have been inclined to build hedgerows) because he
knew the self at the core of his being — a self that rested clearly
in God. In Bolt's play, when More's daughter Meg begs him to
take the oath, More answers:

> When a man takes an oath, Meg, he's holding his own self in
> his own hands. Like water. And if he opens his fingers then —
> he needn't hope to find himself again. Some men aren't
> capable of this, but I'd be loath to think your father one of
> them. (Bolt, p. 81)

What are the stepping stones of More's love life that might
illuminate how he grounded himself in God so deeply that he
greeted life and death with generosity and grace?

1. Thomas More was one of six children of a prosperous
judge who married four times (the last time at seventy) and who
sent Thomas to live as a child with the Archbishop of
Canterbury, John Morton, where Thomas learned not only
Latin but courtly ways. Morton said of the child More, "This
child waiting at the table, whosoever live to see it, will prove a
marvelous man."

2. A fine student, More studied law at Oxford and lived in
simplicity and some poverty on the small allowance his father
gave him. In his young manhood, he was attracted to the
religious life and lived with the Carthusians for three years,
where he came to love silence and fasting. His religious superiors

advised him not to continue at the monastery. But throughout his busy life he gave long hours to religious exercises, Mass, prayers and psalms, recited with his household. Even when he became Lord Chancellor he wore under his gorgeous robes a hairshirt that chafed and bloodied his body.

3. When twenty years old, he decided to marry his first wife, Jane, choosing — as Erasmus thought — "to be a chaste husband rather than a licentious priest." By Jane he had three daughters and one son whose education he oversaw with great care. The girls were tutored in Greek and Latin as well as any men. His eldest daughter Meg was his favorite and the tenderness of their love is apparent in the letters he wrote before his death. When his wife died, leaving him with four young children to raise, he married Dame Alice, a widow with one child, a month after Jane's funeral.

4. After finishing his law degree, he was elected to parliament where he resisted Henry VII's exorbitant tax demands, and so had to flee to the continent for awhile. He became a brilliant scholar, the finest in England; he wrote *Utopia*, became a friend to other leading thinkers — Erasmus; John Colet, Dean of St. Paul's, the most important leader of English Humanism; William Lily, Greek scholar; Thomas Linacre, founder of the Royal College of Physicians.

5. He was ambassador, then judge — a most fair judge. One of the verses of the time said:

> When *More* some time had chancellor been
> No more suits did remain;
> The same shall never more be seen
> Till *More* be there again.

His house at Chelsea was open to the world. Hans Holbein lived with him for two years and left telling portraits of him and his family.

6. At Cardinal Wolsey's failure to please Henry VIII in obtaining a divorce from Catherine of Aragon so he could wed Anne Boleyn, More became Lord Chancellor of the realm. It was then that Henry would visit him at Chelsea, his arm draped over More's shoulder. Sir Thomas More (for he had been knighted in 1521) knew well the ambivalent gift the king's familiar arm would prove; as he indicated to his son-in-law Roper, who had married Meg:

> Howbeit son Roper, I may tell thee I have no cause to be proud thereof; for if my head could win him a castle in France . . . it should not fail to go.

7. After Henry's marriage to Anne Boleyn, there swiftly followed the Act of Supremacy to which all were asked to give allegiance by oath. More resigned his chancellorship and prepared his family for poverty. "Now we will all have to live as I lived as a student in Oxford," he said. He found positions for all his servants, though his jester who loved him well had to be carried away by force. He also prepared them for his imprisonment, staging rehearsals of that time when an official would come to carry him away through Traitor's Gate. When the moment finally came, he closed the garden gate and would not let his wife and children watch him embark. His family pleaded with him then, as later in the long year he languished in prison, not to scruple over the oath which all the lords of the realm and all the bishops in England had taken, save only Bishop John Fisher.

The integrity of More's conscience shines never so clearly as here where he condemned no one who had taken the oath. He begged his family to try to understand that he could do no other.

They were allowed to visit him in prison, if they would promise to try to persuade him to take the oath. He held firm against these, the most difficult encroachments of love.

8. At first he used the time in prison to read and write but then all books and paper were taken from him. After the trial where Richard Rich perjured himself to swear that More had spoken against the king, More knew that his fate was set. In the solemn procession back to the tower, with the executioner's axe turned toward him, he blessed for the last time his son John More who fell at his father's feet. He comforted too, Sir William Kingston, head of the guards, who was leading him back, and who wept to see More blessing his son.

> At the tower Margaret, heavy with child, and without consideration or care of herself, passing through the midst of the throng and guard of men, who with bills and halberds compassed him about, there openly in the sight of them all, embraced him, took him about the neck and kissed him, not able to say any word but, "Oh, my Father. Oh, my Father." He gave her his fatherly blessing, telling her that whatsoever he should suffer, though he were innocent, it was not without the will of God, and therefore she must be patient for her loss. After separation she, 'all ravaged with entire love of her dear father, suddenly turned back again, ran to him as before, took him about the neck and divers times together most lovingly kissed him,' a sight which made even the guards weep and mourn. (Farrow, p. 223, quoting from William Roper)

It was for Margaret the day before he died that he took up his piece of coal and scratched his last letter, telling her to say his farewells and blessings to friends and dispose of a few possessions. The letter reads in part:

. . . and therefore tomorrow long I to go to God; it were a day very meet and convenient for me. I never liked your manner toward me better than when you kissed me last; for I love when daughterly love and dear charity hath no leisure to look to worldly courtesy. Farewell, my dear child, and pray for me, and I shall for you and all your friends so that we may merrily meet in heaven.

By mercy from the king, Thomas was not to be hanged and quartered, but merely beheaded. When given this information he said he hoped that "none of his friends might experience the like mercy from the king." He was further forbidden by the king to speak many words at his execution. Thomas obeyed.

I am ready obediently to conform myself to his grace's commandments. And I beseech you, Master Pope, to be a mean unto his Highness that my daughter Margaret may be at my burial.

Master Pope too broke down and wept at More's gratitude on hearing that all his family would be allowed to attend the burial. When More was not able to comfort Pope, he wittily picked up his urinal, as if a doctor examining it for disease (as was the custom) and said professionally, "I see no danger but that this man may live longer if it please the king." Like Christ his good master, he sought to comfort those distraught by his death.

Dressed in a rough robe and carrying a red cross, he went before the vast mob assembled to watch him die. They eagerly waited for his last speech, but obediently his words were brief, asking the crowd to pray for him and to bear witness that he was dying "in and for the faith of the Holy Catholic Church" and that he died "the king's good servant, but God's first." He knelt and recited the "Miserere"; he comforted the executioner as he gave him the customary gold coin and said:

> Pluck up thy spirit, man, and be not afraid to do thy office; my neck is very short; take heed, therefore, that thou strike not awry for saving of thy honesty.

When More had said his last joke about saving his beard for it had never offended the king, the executioner struck cleanly. More's head rolled off, was taken up and posted on London Bridge for all to see for the next month. His beloved Meg risked her life to row under the bridge one night to receive this beloved rotting head, thrown down from the bridge by a bribed guard.

If how we die is some sort of witness to how we have lived, there are few deaths as compelling as More's. First he died for a truth he clearly saw because he had somehow loved it into the marrow of his bones, so that when the externals of supports of his life were honed down, the truth and his self were one. How difficult it is for many even to conceive of a truth that one would die for today.

The brilliance of his witty mind could honor the ambiguities of the situation he found himself in, so he could condemn no man for taking the oath. One is tempted to take the ambiguities which ornament the context of truth as excuses for not living it, loving it, or dying for it. More knew many corrupt Churchmen; he had been an ambassador and politician — he knew that the Church's stance regarding Henry's annulment from Catherine of Aragon could be easily read another way, were Spain not so important to the pope. But in the end he knew surely that, despite the shortcomings of institutions, no man could, like Henry, be a law unto himself. More's strength came from living love and law — not as contraries but helpers, one to the other. Henry broke the law so that he could have the love of Anne; in breaking the law, love ultimately vanished. When the news of the execution was taken to Henry, he was playing cards with Anne Boleyn. "You are the cause of this man's death," he said and left her abruptly.

Fine lawyer that he was, and pray-er, More knew the limits of law, the aim of law: to fence in a space where love could grow. The fierce scene of love between father and daughter before which the hardened guard wept has few parallels in history. One cannot presume that the profound marriage of love and law which More had accomplished in his life was an easy one, for with the last love letter he wrote to Margaret he sent the hairshirt he always wore, and she always washed — their secret from the world.

> *O St. Thomas More, wonderful father, jester, writer, friend and lover, lawyer, ascetic who loved and lived so abundantly, help me not to fear the abundance to which God calls me; help me to find the laws of love, the haven hairshirts, the strange and wondrous objects which will lure me away from fear of my own emptiness in all the seasons of my life. Help me to laugh wittily at my daily deaths, to comfort tenderly those confused by pain, to speak of the future life in such a way that all who hear may believe its reality. May I meet you merrily on earth as well as in heaven; may I bring you to all the clashes of church and politics I suffer from; may I bring your genius of friendship to all my loves, content like you, to be a busy lover in the Lord, a dutiful marriage broker of law and love.*

FOR PERSONAL REFLECTION

1. Write a description of your social context, where you labor and love. What prevents you from plunging deeply into it, loving it, serving it, as Sir Thomas More loved and served his social context?

2. What are the encroachments of others that you find hardest to resist? Why for you is it hard to resist the encroachments of your loved ones?

3. What physical asceticisms do you practice now? Have you ever practiced? Who do you know who has combined asceticism with love of life?

4. Sir Thomas More loved beautiful things and the good life, as descriptions of his home at Chelsea indicate. Describe any home you have ever lived in that brought happiness to all who came there. Why do you think Erasmus called the felicity (happiness) at Chelsea a fatal felicity?

5. Do you have a good sense of humor? What are the areas that you find it difficult to laugh at? Why do you imagine that joyfulness is an essential attribute of sanctity?

6. What do you find most attractive about More's life? What nourishes you in his story? Discourages you?

7. When have you, or a relative of yours, taken a stand in conscience which no one else understood? What stories have you ever been told by parents or teachers that encouraged you to take unpopular stands? When you stand alone, do you condemn as cowards those who don't follow *your* conscience?

8. Law serves as the protector and container of love. When, in your life experience, has law failed to serve love?

9. Where in your life do you need to bring witty words; where, asceticism; where, deep moral sensitivity to your own conscience; where, forgiveness of others who do not follow your lights; where, abundant love for your family and your social context?

10. Meg was More's favorite child. This favor meant for her special love and deep suffering. Have you ever been someone's favorite? Do you think it is possible for a parent not to have a favorite child?

11. How important are friendships to your spiritual life? More had in a true sense become a friend to his daughter. With which of your relatives have you become a friend?

12. Thomas More was both virtuous and lovable. Who is the most virtuous person you know? The most lovable? Why are these qualities hard to find in one person?

ST. TERESA of AVILA (1515-1582)

Ronda Chervin

St. Teresa of Avila, Spanish contemplative nun, reformer of the Carmelite Order, writer of spiritual books, Doctor of the Church, is of all the saints, the one I identify with most.

I also come from a Spanish and Jewish background on one side of my family. I am also strong of will, yet relatively weak of body; friendly and chatty, yet longing for silence and solitude; bold, yet loving to take advice from authorities; passionately eager for spiritual friendship and also for total union with God. When I read Teresa's *Life,* her *Interior Castle,* or the *Way of Perfection,* I hope that I would have written in exactly the same way had I been a Carmelite sister of the 16th century; and I imagine she might write the way I do, were she in my place.

That is not to deny the differences: I am a wife and mother and professor, not a Carmelite. She had virtues I have never come close to possessing: it is said that she never complained even when enduring extreme physical suffering or when battling to fulfill God's will against the opposition of the most powerful prelates of her time. These virtues came from the trust she placed in divine providence; and that trust, in turn, came from an extraordinary prayer-life, giving her that same sure confidence in God's will to be found in Catherine of Siena and Paul of Tarsus. It was her accounts of her mystical relationship to Christ which first attracted me to the saint whose books are second in popularity in Spain only to *Don Quixote*.

It was through her books that the idea first came into my mind that a human being could be as close to God as to a human lover; that religion could be ecstatic and God companionable. The fact that Teresa was a reluctant saint, one who originally took vows without much enthusiasm, one who was for years torn between the joys of prayer, and the more human delights of conversation in the parlor — all this gave hope to one like myself coming to the Church with such a poor preparation.

Joseph Glynn, O.C.D., a priest of the Carmelite order, includes in his recent book *The Eternal Mystic* some inspiring comments by contemporaries about Teresa's character:

"Fray Pedro Fernandez, Provincial of the Spanish Dominican Province, a legally minded man, very chary of false mystics . . . in the end came around and said that after all Teresa of Jesus was a holy woman which, in the mouth of this Master was praise indeed. . . . Another master of the same order once (said) 'Who is this Teresa of Jesus. . . . One cannot trust women's virtue, you know'. . . . He went to Toledo and heard her confession nearly every day and tested her quite severely. When this witness next met him, (he) answered jokingly: 'Oh, you had deceived me for you said she was a woman; upon my word she is a man, a real strong man.'" (Glynn, p. 17)

"Mother Ana de la Encarnacion knew Teresa for thirty years and had this to say:

'She always saw great simplicity and humility in Madre Teresa de Jesus and in spite of being the foundress of all these monasteries she did not wish to exercise any authority in any houses she happened to be in. On the contrary she would serve in the refectory, cook in the kitchen, . . . She was fond of taking advice and would take it from the youngest in the house. . . . On another occasion it happened that a provincial took exception to her, sent her a command under pain of excommunication that she would leave the monastery in Medina with the Prioress who was there. This order arrived very late on a very cold night and they left straightaway, for the sake of obeying. She suffered very much on the way owing to the extreme cold and because she had paralysis and other ailments. Yet, with all she went happily and cheerfully. . . .' " (Glynn, p. 18)

Another companion states that "So great and continuous was her prayer and her realization of the presence of God that to be able to stand it (without dying of ecstasy) she had to be absorbed and attend to external affairs pertaining to the Rule and increase of the houses of the Order. Moreover, she used to communicate to God her business affairs and he used to talk to her and tell her many things concerning her foundations, with far more familiarity than one reads of in the case of other Saints." (Glynn, p. 20)

Nothing that has been written about Teresa, however, can compare to her own wonderful, familiar style of recounting her experiences. I will quote for you some of my favorite passages, but first, will give you a description of her appearance and a bit more about her life so that you can understand the passages in context.

"She was of medium height, tended to be more plump than thin. Her unusual face could not be described as either round or aquiline. . . . Her forehead was broad, her eyebrows somewhat thick . . . her eyes were black, lively and round, not very large, but well placed, protruding a little. The nose was small, the mouth — medium in size and delicately shaped. . . . The white teeth sparkled and were equal in size." (St. Teresa, *Collected Works*, Vol. II, p. 12)

This description corresponds pretty well to the print I have on my wall of a painting by an anonymous artist. In this famous picture she is dressed in her habit and her eyes are uplifted with an expression both intense and entranced.

I heard a humorous and endearing anecdote about Teresa's own reaction to sitting for her portrait. When it was finished and she saw it for the first time, she remarked, "May God forgive you, you have succeeded in making me look ugly." I was very consoled to think that even women saints fit into Hamlet's famous indictment "vanity, thy name is woman."

Teresa was the third daughter in a large Spanish family of the upper class. She was a very lively, much favored child, and was sent away to a convent school after the death of her mother, most likely because of her flirtatious tendencies.

The idea of a religious vocation was not particularly appealing to the vivacious young woman who had many possible suitors, but the notion of marriage was even less so, for she had witnessed her mother's fatigue and had no desire to duplicate such a life.

She chose to enter a convent which she thought to be the most lax, for in those days many girls of the upper classes joined religious communities as a way of extending the irresponsibility of youth. They practiced a bare minimum of devotion to God, and spent the rest of the time visiting with relatives and friends in the parlor.

Various influences, however, worked to introduce Teresa to a deeper prayer life. She began to experience intermittent contemplative recollection and even moments of union with Christ, but she hesitated to give herself totally to the divine. No matter how she struggled against it, the pull of the parlor would win out. It took her some twenty years during which she was gifted with beautiful ecstasies, locutions and raptures, before she was able to break with her desire for human fellowship and seek the seclusion that could only be available in convents reformed according to the older Carmelite ways. The founding of such convents became her life-work.

Here is a passage typical of her autobiography analyzing the reasons for her difficulty in choosing Christ alone as her companion:

"I had a serious fault, which led me into great trouble. It was that if I began to realize that a person liked me, and I took to him myself, I would grow so fond of him that my memory would feel compelled to revert to him and I would always be thinking of him; without intentionally giving any offence to God. I would delight in seeing him and think about him and his good qualities. This was such a harmful thing that it was ruining my soul.

"But when once I had seen the great beauty of the Lord (in a vision) I saw no one who by comparison with Him seemed acceptable to me on whom my thoughts wished to dwell. . . . Nor is there any knowledge of any kind of consolation to which I can attach the slightest esteem by comparison with that which it causes me to hear a single word coming from that Divine mouth. . . . And, unless for my sins the Lord allows this memory to fade, I consider it impossible for me to be so deeply absorbed in anything that I do not regain my freedom when I turn once more in thought, even for a moment, to this Lord." (St. Teresa, *Life*, p. 262)

Once sequestered in her reformed Carmelite convent, and brought into still greater union with Christ, she was able to enjoy inspiring spiritual friendships without any distraction to prayer.

Having had many such friendships myself, some of which were disastrous, others full of sorrow, even in the midst of joy, I found this passage most enlightening. The problem, as I see it, lies in the great difference between being very religious and being in union with God. Praying often, going to Church frequently, trying to love one's neighbor as oneself, etc. can give one the illusion that God is the true center of one's life. It may be true that one wishes that God was the center, but at the same time, on an emotional level, one may still be craving a "perfect" human love. This leads to inflated appraisals of the virtues of beloved friends, and a strong tendency to long for the fruition of such relationships, even contrary to God's will.

It is only when two individuals have achieved much healing of the heart that they can accept the sacrifices entailed in spiritual friendships for the sake of fidelity to the powerful, loving presence of Christ, Himself, as their ultimate lover.

To return to the life of St. Teresa:

The founding of reformed convents was no easy matter in those troubled times of European history. Because of the inroads of Protestantism, together with the flourishing of many brands of false mysticism, Church authorities were extremely wary of allowing priests or sisters to put into effect plans "given directly from on high."

Not only were some of the reformed Carmelites thrown into jail, as was St. John of the Cross, but there was always fear of the Inquisition. Perhaps still worse, endless complicated negotiations were required each time a small group of nuns expressed the desire to move from an affluent, "acceptable" convent of the relaxed rule, to a poor, "enclosed" house.

Often at the point of giving up, Teresa would be forced onward by the clear instructions given to her by her Lord and King during prayer.

By the time of her death at the age of 67, she had founded more than fifteen reformed convents and houses for women and men. She died in a holy manner described in this way by Anne of St. Bartholomew, one of the sisters:

"Just before she died Our Lord was at the foot of the bed. . . . The glorious splendour emanating from Our Lord formed a kind of canopy . . . (Teresa) died leaving a strong and pleasant fragrance in the whole room. . . . The body of the holy Mother had turned so transparent and shining that it seemed as if one could see oneself in her hands. . . . She (Anne) believes that what finally caused her death was that her ardent and fervent desire and love for Our Lord and God and her anxiety to be with

Him and enjoy Him weakened and enfeebled her. . . . When the Blessed Sacrament was brought to her, so great was her joy and happiness when she saw Him, that if she had not been prevented she would have thrown herself out of bed and with so much fervour and desire that it seemed as if her soul were rushing out after his Divine Majesty." (Glynn, p. 19)

What is the secret of St. Teresa? How live so that one dies in such a way? Great as the hospice movement is by comparison to the usual hospital death, no amount of tranquilizers or human comfort can provide a death such as the one just described.

The key, for Teresa, lay in total openness in prayer. Before outlining for you Teresa's teaching on prayer, I would like to give some random excerpts to summon you into the intense, yet very natural mood of Teresa's communication with Christ and of His with her:

"You are Teresa of Jesus, I am Jesus of Teresa." (St. Teresa, *Life*, p. 343)

"Labour not to hold Me enclosed within thyself, but to enclose thyself within Me." (St. Teresa, *Life*, p. 343)

"A few days after . . . while I was wondering if the people were right who disapproved of my going out to make foundations and if I should do better to occupy myself continually in prayer, I heard these words: 'For as long as life lasts, there is no gain to be had in striving to have greater fruition of Me. But only in doing My will. . . . Ask them (those who blocked Teresa) if they will be able to tie My hands.' " (St. Teresa, *Life*, p. 344)

"Thou seemest, Lord, to give severe tests to those who love Thee, but only that in the extremity of their trials they may learn the greater extremity of Thy love." (St. Teresa, *Life*, p. 163)

"Let us be mad for the love of Him who was called mad for our sakes." (St. Teresa, *Life*, p. 99)

"I lost all trust in myself and was placing all my confidence in God. . . . I believe I told Him then that I would not rise from the spot until He had granted me only to do His will." (St. Teresa, *Life*, p. 54)

And, for a change of mood:

"I often tell you, sisters, . . . not to forget that we in this house, and for that matter anyone who would be perfect, must flee a thousand leagues from such phrases as: 'I had right on my side;' 'they had no right to do this to me' . . . God deliver us from such a false idea of right as that! Do you think that it was right for our good Jesus to have to suffer so many insults, and that those who heaped them on Him were right. . . . I do not know why anyone is in a convent who is willing to bear only the crosses she has a perfect right to expect: such a person should return to the world, though even there such rights will not be safeguarded. . . . To desire to share in the Kingdom, and to enjoy it, and yet not to be willing to have any part in His dishonors and trials, is ridiculous." (St. Teresa, *Way of Perfection*, pp. 53-54)

I do not take this last passage, which sounds so modern, to mean that Teresa would disapprove of wholesome assertiveness. She was certainly sturdy in defense of her convictions. I think she means rather, a complaining way of quarreling about rights in situations where no good outcome is possible.

After this appetizer, let us turn to the teachings on prayer that have made Teresa not only a delightfully readable saint but also a Doctor of the Church.

Teresa's two most famous metaphors describing stages in prayer are the analogy of drawing water and the image of the mansions of the interior castle. The water image is the simpler of the two.

The first stage in prayer, meditation, is described as drawing water from the well. (St. Teresa, *Life*, p. 66 ff.) In *meditation*, as opposed to *contemplation* (note that these words are not synonymous, though they are often considered so in ordinary parlance), we do most of the work. We have to send down a bucket, so to speak, by deciding on a religious topic to ponder.

We have to think about this subject and draw out inspiration from it. During this stage of prayer a person would normally be concerned in daily life with getting rid of worldliness.

The second stage is likened to a water wheel. Just as water can be drawn from the source without effort when there is a water wheel to do the work, so in the second stage, which is contemplation, there is no work to be done by the person at prayer. Instead, the peace of the Lord descends to bring quiet over the soul. As explained by Poulain in his classic work, *The Graces of Interior Prayer*, what distinguishes meditation from contemplation is that, in the case of the latter, there is no way that we can bring such a state on ourselves by our own efforts. It is pure grace coming from God. It comes through the Holy Spirit, when He wills. Yet we can ask in our vocal prayer that such graces be given, for Jesus promises us the peace that passes all understanding, and most of us have very little of this peace.

The third stage is similar to the waters of a brook which overflows in a bubbling fashion. In this stage of prayer, praise wells up in the soul causing shouts of joy and words without rhyme or reason. (St. Teresa, *Life*, p. 97) Teresa calls this a holy madness. One presumes that she was experiencing the gift of tongues.

The fourth and last stage is described as rain. In this stage grace descends like rain to fill all the faculties. One moment of such prayer is worth all the trials of a lifetime. These gifts make the soul very strong and brave. It is in this period of prayer that many experience trances, raptures, elevations, locutions, and a great sense of closeness to Christ as the Bridegroom of the soul. Yet all is not bliss, for the very extremity of joy coming during the peak times, is followed by loneliness, a burning longing for God, and a terrible sense of one's own sinfulness when failing to love God and neighbor in the manner which seems the proper response after so great an experience of the Source of all love.

Many years ago when first reading such descriptions of contemplation I was amazed at the infinite vistas awaiting me. Very occasionally, about once a year, I would have a flashing vision of Christ. I would treasure such moments, finding solace in them for all the weary times of dry, rote prayer.

Now, having come into some, if not all, of the gifts of prayer Teresa describes, I am amazed at the simplicity of her explanations, for this is a sphere so mysterious and frightening that it is impossible to imagine beforehand the sufferings peculiar to it. The remedies given by St. Teresa are among the best in the literature of spirituality.

The second famous image of the interior crystal castle given to St. Teresa during a vision, I found similar to our contemporary use of the word "space." We speak of ourselves or others as having moved into "another space." "I'm in a different space now," we tell our friends, meaning by space a new sense of reality.

Teresa wrote, "I began to think of the soul as if it were a castle made of a single diamond or of very clear crystal, in which there are many rooms just as in Heaven there are many mansions." (St. Teresa, *Interior Castle*, p. 201)

"Would it not be a sign of great ignorance, my daughters, if a person were asked who he was, and could not say, and had no idea who his father or his mother was, or from what country he came? Though that is great stupidity, our own is incomparably greater if we make no attempt to discover what we are, and only know that we are living in these bodies, and have a vague idea, because we have heard it and because our Faith tells us so, that we possess souls. As to what good qualities there may be in our souls, or Who dwells within them, or how precious they are — those things which we seldom consider and so we trouble little about carefully preserving the soul's beauty. All our interest is centered in the rough setting of the diamond, and in the outer wall of the castle — that is to say, in these bodies of ours. Let us now imagine that this castle, . . . contains many mansions, some above, others below, others at each side; and in the center and midst of them all is the chiefest mansion where the most secret things pass between God and the soul." (St. Teresa, *Interior Castle*, pp. 201-202)

Now I will give a very short summary of the nature of each of Teresa's set of mansions together with a few of her own lines to make the explanation more vivid. It should be noted that Teresa spoke of each spiritual space as a set of mansions, plural, for she by no means desired to convey the impression that there was a rigid, standard method of arriving at union with God.

The First Mansions

Outside the castle there are venomous reptiles symbolizing the sins of the world. Many people are too involved with these sins to even enter the castle. But those who begin to seek to be closer to God in prayer are said to have entered the first mansions. It is still rather dark inside, for fascination with sin blocks the light.

"At this early stage, as the soul is still absorbed in worldly affairs, engulfed in worldly pleasure and puffed up with worldly honors and ambitions, its vassals, which are the senses . . . have not the same power, and such a soul is easily vanquished . . . take every opportunity to repairing to His majesty, and make His blessed mother their intercessor . . . so that these may do battle for them. . . ." (St. Teresa, *Interior Castle*, p. 210)

I am going to frame my reaction to each of Teresa's mansions in the form of a prayer.

Lord Jesus, I thank you that I am no longer in these first mansions. For the most part, the world with all its greed and pride appalls me. And yet, to my great shame, occasionally I lose all sight of the heavenly horizon and hanker after some paltry

thing as if it were You, Yourself. I shout at a child who blocks the
TV when I am watching some show, the theme of which may be
an amusing, intriguing aspect of sin. I rage and fret if someone
takes the last piece of bacon from the refrigerator. I know, Lord,
that You are all merciful and, that far from scorning me for such
failings, You are laughing at me merrily. I beg You, Lord, to
purify me from such inconsistencies, for I would be free from all
that is not of Your Kingdom.

The Second Mansions

In the second mansions are to be found those who seek
every chance to advance in love of God and neighbor. They seek
the company of the good, receive the sacraments, pray often.
There is much more warmth and light in these mansions than in
the first.

"These souls, then, can understand the Lord when He calls
them; for, as they gradually get nearer to the place where His
Majesty dwells, He becomes a very good neighbor to them. And
such are His mercy and goodness that, even when we are
engaged in our worldly pastimes and businesses and pleasures
and hagglings, when we are falling into sins and rising from
them again . . . in spite of all that, this Lord of ours is so anxious
that we should desire Him and strive after His companionship
that He calls us ceaselessly." (St. Teresa, *Interior Castle*, pp.
213-214)

The way God speaks to us in these mansions is not by way
of locutions but more often through the words of good people or
from books, or from trials.

In the meantime the Devil is at work particularly by trying
to "show the soul . . . the things of the world — and they pretend
that earthly pleasures are almost eternal." (St. Teresa, *Interior
Castle*, p. 214)

The remedy for these temptations comes from the Holy Spirit inspiring us to realize how superior God's love is to earthly pleasures. "For the world is full of falsehood and these pleasures which the devil pictures to it are accompanied by trials and cares and annoyances." (St. Teresa, *Interior Castle*, p. 215) It is also extremely important at this stage to associate with those who are also striving for union with God, and some who are more advanced so that we may be spurred on by the sight of the peace and joy to be had at the end of the journey.

Oh my Jesus, how stupid I still am, and a professor of Christian philosophy at that! Still, in fantasy, the Devil presents me with images of the great peace I would attain if only I gave up projects undertaken for the sake of the Kingdom. Still, he can make sin seem fascinating, and virtue unbearable. "The spirit is willing but the flesh is weak." Happily you have sent me wonderful, holy friends to lead me forward. May I never be without such friends! Most of all, draw me close to You so that the experience of Your beauty may show me how false are the pleasures of giving up on God.

The Third Mansions

These are the abodes of those who are highly virtuous, yet not totally surrendered to God. Because of their victory over mortal sin, with the help of grace, there is danger of complacency and self-righteousness. In these mansions there are occasional glimpses of the King, but there is also much aridity — dryness in prayer.

When we become bored by aridity we must remember, Teresa tells us, that Our Lord Himself did nothing but serve, without asking for gifts or favors. "Be sure that, where there is true humility, even if God never grants the soul favors, He will give it peace and resignation to His will . . . " (St. Teresa, *Interior*

Castle, pp. 221-223) Often such favors are given to the weak to encourage them, so no one should feel proud because of them.

In one of her more famous passages Teresa warns against complacency setting in during this stage: "Their love is not yet ardent enough to overwhelm their reason. How I wish ours would make us dissatisfied with this habit of always serving God at a snail's pace!" (St. Teresa, *Interior Castle*, pp. 226-227)

Remedies suggested by Teresa for moving out of the third mansions consist of seeking good spiritual direction and being obedient to the director, and also avoiding absolutely the tendency to find fault with others. Silence is highly advised.

How this description alarms me! For many years I dwelled in these mansions, Lord. Yes, truly I was fulfilling my obligations as a Catholic with greater precision than many, but how hard my heart could be! How much more real virtue there was in many who were less anxious to fulfill the letter of the law. Happily, You began to bring me out of this state through the release of charismatic prayer with its emphasis on praise and freedom in the Spirit. May I never become hard again in my attempt to be virtuous. "Melt my heart and make it like unto Thine."

The Fourth Mansions

In these rooms grace flows from God in a new manner. The experiences here correspond to the "water-wheel" phase where infused prayer of quiet takes the place of studied meditation. Inhabitants of the fourth mansions have no interest in worldly things, so entranced are they with the things of God. They shrink from no trials and therefore are capable of much greater love of neighbor.

". . . if you would progress a long way on this road and ascend to the Mansions of your desire, the important thing is not to think much, but to love much; do, then, whatever most arouses you to love. Perhaps we do not know what love is: it would not surprise me a great deal to learn this, for love consists, not in the extent of our happiness, but in the firmness of our determination to try to please God in everything, and to endeavor, in all possible ways, not to offend Him, and to pray Him ever to advance the honor and glory of His Son and the growth of the Catholic Church." (St. Teresa, *Interior Castle*, p. 233)

In the fourth mansions we experience what the psalmist called "the enlargement of the heart." "The heavenly water begins to flow from our very depths — it proceeds to spread within it and cause an interior (enlargement) . . . and ineffable blessings, so that the soul itself cannot understand all that it receives there." (St. Teresa, *Interior Castle*, pp. 237-238)

The soul seems to be withdrawing into itself as does a turtle. It has firm confidence in being saved from the dangers of hell.

This stage can be dangerous, however. Apparently St. Teresa had experiences with sisters of weak body and mind who would drift from the "prayer of quiet" into a state of somnambulance. In such cases our always practical guide recommends a return to a more active life with good nourishment.

My God, I bless and praise You for choosing to bring me into this mansion in spite of all my sins and faults. I, who never thought to experience a moment of peace, have been given this gift now most frequently. What rest for my hagridden psyche! I pray that You may ever be with me in this manner, for my nature is so nervous that without Your grace in prayer I am much hindered in my work, for all are confused at the sight of someone dedicated to You being so tense. So, for the sake of my family and students and all I meet, as well as for my own benefit, I implore You to give me the graces of this Mansion for the rest of my life.

The Fifth Mansions

It is very hard for the reader to understand at first why Teresa separates what she calls the fifth and the sixth mansions. The sixth is the engagement period. The fifth is more like what we would call "going steady."

It is in this part of the interior castle that many experience trances and a simple sense of union. What takes place in these short periods of self-loss cannot be described in words but is yet very precious. The joy that comes in such moments is quite delicate, and greater than any to be found in human activities or states of heart. It penetrates "the very marrow of the bones." (St. Teresa, *Interior Castle*, p. 250)

A mark of these mansions is that the person receiving such gifts can have no doubt whatsoever that they come from God. Just as Christ came to the disciples after the Resurrection without using a door, so does He come into the soul without stirring the intellect or the will. (St. Teresa, *Interior Castle*, p. 252)

There is a new kind of suffering in these mansions. Because the self is much more identified with Christ it feels much more pain at the knowledge of how little God is loved in the world and also at the thought of so many people being far from the graces God wishes to give them because of their preference for sin. Merely thinking about such matters before coming into this mansion "does not reach to the depths of our being, as does this grief, which, without any effort on the soul's part, and sometimes against its will, seems to tear it to pieces and grind it to powder." (St. Teresa, *Interior Castle*, p. 257)

It would seem that there could be no falling back after such inundations of grace, and yet St. Teresa warns that betrayals are still possible. To avoid such Judas behavior, we must keep obedient to the law of God, especially in love of neighbor.

My God, how these words make me shudder. Have I not been acquainted with deeply contemplative people who seemed to enjoy trance-like states of union with You, who have suddenly rid themselves of the crosses of their state in life, falling into the sin of betraying their loved ones? How difficult it sometimes is to move from the glory of union with You in prayer, into the "petty" environment of daily existence! Immediately after immersion in Your heart in prayer I am ready for any trial, but a few hours afterwards everything seems irksome to me and I find myself relishing dreams of escape even as I battle against such images. Since I have not a single natural virtue, I insist that You, who have brought me this far, infuse in me the love for serving others no matter what the cost.

The Sixth Mansions

It is in these rooms that many come into such graces as raptures, locutions, levitations, and interior visions. It is as if the Divine Lover cannot wait for the marital bond to be sealed and rushes to give her every gift to show His love.

Yet, here again, there are dreadful crosses to be endured such as ridicule, calumny, fear of self-deceit, and a great love for death as the transition to consummation.

"For this is another of the great trials suffered by these souls, especially if they have been wicked — namely, to think that because of their sins God will permit them to be deceived (to have false visions and locutions) — and although, when His majesty grants them this favor, they feel secure and cannot believe that it comes from any other spirit than a spirit of God, yet, as it is a state which passes quickly, and the soul is ever mindful of its sins, and it sees faults in itself for these are never lacking — it then begins to suffer this torture." (St. Teresa, *Interior Castle*, p. 272)

Against such difficulties there is no remedy except from God Himself who can suddenly, with a single word or chance occasion, remove all these troubles.

However, we are not to accept any vision or locution as absolutely certain without the advice of a spiritual director. In this way we are safe from being misled by the imagination or the Devil. The desire for death increases now, in the words of Teresa's famous poem "Dying that I do not die."

I thank You, Lord, for sending me these words of Your great saint. Since beginning to receive some intimations of the gifts of the sixth mansions, I have been tortured by the feeling that such graces could not possibly be given in truth to a person with so many obvious flaws — I mean irritability, uncontrolled anger, vengeful thoughts. The fear that all these experiences of You are really the result of a fevered imagination, some kind of psychosis, or the Devil's work, is never far from me except, as Teresa says, when actually being immersed in Your being in prayer. I cannot wish, glorious God, that You would take away the graces of interior prayer, for they are too sublime to be renounced. Instead I wish that You would take away those flaws which stand out so hideously against the background of Your goodness.

The Seventh Mansions

Finally we arrive at the goal of our journey through the interior castle — the complete union, as far as this is possible in time, between the human spirit and its beloved Creator: the spiritual marriage.

Lest this image seem sentimental we should bear in mind that for St. Teresa it was firmly based on the Scripture: "Even as thou, Father, art in me, and I in thee, that they also may be in us." (John 17:21)

Describing her own experience of the spiritual marriage, Teresa tells how it was ushered in by means of an interior vision of the Trinity followed by one of the Sacred Humanity of the Lord in the splendor of His Resurrection. He told her that from that point on she should take His affairs upon her as her own and He would do the like for her. (St. Teresa, *Interior Castle*, p. 334)

If this message sounds pedestrian, it is well to consider what it would mean in our own lives to completely cast aside all care for our own future, leaving it in the hands of an omniscient, omnipotent Lover.

The spiritual marriage differs from the engagement phase described in the chapters about the sixth mansions, for now as in human marriages the two have become one, and there is no more separation. The engagement is compared to two candles held close so that their flames join. In this case the candles can still be pulled apart afterwards. But in the marriage the image is of "rain falling from the heavens into a river or a spring; there is nothing but water there and it is impossible to divide or separate the water belonging to the river from that which fell from the heavens." (St. Teresa, *Interior Castle*, p. 335)

Now the human soul has entered into the mansion of the beloved. From now on, the innermost part of the soul is in deep peace, although outwardly there can still be great distress from a variety of causes, the greatest of which is the sight of its own imperfections, which persist involuntarily in spite of the degree of union it has been graced with.

The effects of spiritual marriage are a complete self-forgetfulness, a willingness and even desire to suffer for the Kingdom, joy in the midst of persecution, immediate forgiveness of enemies, a great fervor in helping others, complete loss of the fear of death now thought of as a "gentle rapture," detachment from all things but those concerning the Kingdom, no further interior trials. (St. Teresa, *Interior Castle*, pp. 399-341)

As St. Teresa prayed:

"Oh, Jesus! If only one knew how many things there are in Scripture which describe this peace of the soul! My God, since Thou seest how needful it is for us, do Thou inspire Christians to desire to seek it; take it not, by Thy mercy, from those to whom Thou hast given it, and who, until Thou give them true peace and take them where peace will never end, must always live in fear." (St. Teresa, *Interior Castle*, p. 343)

For my part I can only rejoice that there is a stage of marriage beyond my present state of interior suffering where the peace which passes all understanding will be mine in the arms of my God.

In the meantime I will say Teresa's most famous prayer which she used as a bookmark:

> Let nothing disturb thee,
> Let nothing dismay thee.
>
> All things pass.
> God never changes.
>
> Patience attains
> all that it strives for.
>
> He who has God
> finds he lacks nothing.
>
> God alone suffices.

FOR PERSONAL REFLECTION

1. With what aspect of St. Teresa's life do you identify?
2. Of the descriptions of Teresa given by contemporaries, which lines could be said of you, and which not? Does this challenge you in any way?

3. Do you think it is easier to be a nun than a married woman? Explain your answer.
4. How have friendships hindered your closeness to God? How have they helped?
5. How do you imagine your own death? What in your own life presently anticipates a holy death, and what leads you to fear a terrible experience of death?
6. As you read through the stages in prayer given by Teresa in the water carrying image and the analogy of the interior castle, write down your own encounters with God in these modes. When the stage is above the one you have come to, you might write a prayer expressing your desire to enter this mode.
7. Do you have an alternate image of the soul or its journey to God? If so, explain it. You might want to make a drawing to go with it and perhaps send copies to friends.

ST. JOHN of the CROSS (1542-1591)

Ronda Chervin

Juan de Yepes y Alvarez (John of the Cross) was born in 1542 at Fontiveros, Spain, in a small town of Old Castile not far from Avila. His father was a wealthy silk merchant, a fact which leads some biographers to guess that he came from a family of Jewish converts, for most Spaniards in the clothing trade were of Jewish ancestry.

On a business trip, John's father had fallen in love with a poor weaver and married her, in spite of opposition from his family, an opposition so strong that he was disowned and reduced to sharing the poverty of his wife. Did little John inherit from his father the passionate romanticism that marks his own spirituality?

The marriage produced three sons, but shortly after John's birth, his father died, and his mother was left in dire straits. John was educated in a sort of orphanage, where in exchange for educational opportunities he took care of the sacristy of the convent, and later worked at a hospital. He advance to a Jesuit college where he studied grammar, rhetoric, Greek, Latin, and religion.

John of the Cross was a tiny man, less than five feet tall,

dubbed by St. Teresa as half-of-a-monk. The portrait I have seen shows him with huge, dark eyes, a round face, and a sharp nose.

Deeply religious, John became a Carmelite, and before ordination was sent to study at Salamanca, a university of the highest rank. Visitors to Spain should not miss this university town, still conveying the flavor of its glorious past with delightful Spanish inns to relieve the sublimity of the Church architecture.

John was outstanding in philosophy and theology, especially that of St. Thomas Aquinas. His analytic gifts are constantly in evidence in his commentaries on his own lyrical poetry.

It was while visiting his family for the first time as a priest that he met Mother Teresa of Jesus, later St. Teresa of Avila. She was 52 and he 25 at the time. Eager for solitude and prayer, John had been thinking of becoming a Carthusian. Teresa's ideas for strict reform of the Carmelite order were most attractive to him. It was in the reformed order of Discalced (shoeless) Carmelites that he took the name John of the Cross. The members of the reformed order kept hard fasts, abstained from meat, and lived in poor dwellings, enclosed and withdrawn from the world. The monks also performed active works such as preaching, hearing confession, teaching novices, and spiritual direction. John of the Cross became an expert director of souls, helping immeasurably Teresa herself, as well as many other holy nuns. Most of his famous writings were undertaken as an aid to those in his charge. It is staggering to me to think that such works as the *Ascent of Mt. Carmel* were expected to be read by just a few choice souls.

The most colorful part of the life of St. John of the Cross revolves around the efforts to suppress the reform on the part of the religious of the older order. As Teresa began to found more and more houses of nuns and brothers, she gained the support of many Church officials. The Calced group feared that their relaxed rule of life would eventually be repressed entirely. I will not go into the complicated details of the Church politics which ensued, but move on to the extraordinary fact that John of the Cross was to find himself literally imprisoned in the dungeon of an old monastery because of his support of the reforms.

He was locked up in a room six feet wide and ten feet long, with no window. This place was frightfully cold in winter and suffocating in the summer. He was struck with a lash three evenings a week by the members of the community in an effort to make him withdraw his support of Teresa. Since John refused to renounce the reform, he was forced to endure these punishments for nine months. Finally, a kindly jailer was assigned, who gave him fresh clothing and paper and ink. It was then under such stressful conditions that he began to write his famous religious poetry.

One night, he lowered himself by a rope over the huge, castle-like wall of the monastery. He fled to the south of Spain. I was quite surprised to find that the imagery "one dark night . . ." was quite literal in its origins, using the analogy of his escape from his monastery prison as a figure for the inner journey.

It was later, while acting as a director to some nuns of the order that he began to write the long commentaries on his poems known as *The Ascent of Mount Carmel, The Dark Night, The Living Flame of Love, The Spiritual Canticle,* and others. These have become the most widely read and authoritative works on the mystical life in the Church.

The fact that such masterpieces survived the death of John in 1591 is amazing. Controversies arose in his own order, which left John in the "out" group. Being truly a holy man of great detachment, he rejoiced exceedingly at being voted out of the positions of authority which entailed enormous duties, taking him away from his beloved contemplation. Menial labor, however, he never avoided, happily choosing to clean the latrines as an act of humility and charity. Images of another very tiny, holy man from quite another clime come to mind — Gandhi!

It is said that John had a charming personality. He was always joyful and extremely tender, especially to the sick or poor. I found these characterizations heart warming, because I had somehow pictured him as being much more austere. A biographer describes John riding a donkey through Spain to visit the convents for which he was responsible, singing popular love-songs he had learned from the peasants, but with religious words in place of the human love motifs. Often, it is said, he would go into a trance and fall off the donkey. St. Teresa reports that it was hard to have conversation with John about God because he would levitate in the midst of it, and often cause her to do so as well. Readers of a sober-sides spirituality might have to wonder if God does not have a certain penchant for drama.

John was never known to have borne the slightest grudge against anyone, and he seems to have lived indeed at the level of the spiritual marriage he wrote about so ecstatically.

I first came upon the writings of St. John of the Cross some twenty years ago. It was a very difficult time in my life. Married, and the mother of baby twins, my husband became deathly ill with bronchial asthma.

Panicked by his frequent attacks and worn-out by the difficulties of raising twins, I was desperately looking for some new source of spiritual strength. I called upon an old friend, Charles Rich, a lay contemplative and spiritual writer for advice. He had often spoken of the writings of John of the Cross but was reluctant to suggest them to me. The more he spoke of the doubts he had about my reading John's works, the more eager I became to try. Always spiritually ambitious, it galled me that there might be some exalted way of arriving at union with God that I would not be able to try.

The effect of reading the *Ascent of Mount Carmel* for the first time was overwhelming. Never having devoted much time to meditation before, I was stunned when a blanket of deep peace covered my soul, replacing the chronic anxiety and anger I usually felt. For about a month I was able to do all my household chores, take care of the babies, stay up in the night with my husband during his attacks, in sweet resignation to the will of God. Unfortunately, that lovely state wore off, but in such a gradual manner that I did not think to consider whether it was my fault or not.

What remained for a few years was a quite ambiguous attitude for a married woman to adopt, that is, a certain emotional distance from my husband and children. It would be summed up in the idea that God alone mattered and that human beings, though to be enjoyed at odd moments, were primarily crosses to be endured.

Such negativism was never encouraged by anyone, but in the back of my mind, I justified it on the basis of the poorly digested notions I had hastily picked up from reading John of the Cross.

Later, becoming involved in charismatic spirituality, which is a lot more joyful and earthy, and then hearing about Marriage Encounter, I decided that John of the Cross was really for contemplative nuns, brothers, and priests and not the right thing for lay people actively living in the world.

From time to time I would pick him up again. The severity of his doctrines made me shudder, but also made me glad that I had a haven of warm pleasant Christian life within my prayer group. Especially disturbing to me would be the idea that we not only had to renounce the goods of the earth but also had to renounce all spiritual joys lest we become attached to our experience of God more than to God Himself.

Since it is a general rule of meditative reading that one should not force oneself to read anything which causes disturbance and scruples, I would swiftly return *The Complete Works of John of the Cross* to the shelf, where it lay collecting dust. And yet, I could never read the poems or the diagram at the beginning of the *Ascent* without a tremor of recognition and a frightened feeling that here indeed lay a truth I must one day appropriate, or I would remain stuck at a lower plateau rather than on the top of the mountain where I longed to be.

Finally, this year, coming into the truths and experiences of St. John of the Cross more profoundly, I am eager to show you, the reader, what I have seen — what in St. John's path to God delights me and what seems forbidding at first but resolves itself into a true illumination.

In my preface to this book, I suggested that the saints were brilliantly logical. Each holy man and woman appears to have found a clear path to the homeland, God, which is followed with rigorous consistency. What is the logic of St. John of the Cross? I maintain that the key underlying all of his life and works was that the ultimate union with God can only take place in *solitude*.

It is the positive idea of experienced union with God which inspired the saint. Having tasted and embraced God in solitude, his life work was to help others overcome the obstacles to reaching the same goal.

In *The Spiritual Canticle*, he writes:

> He alone, Who also bears
> In solitude the wound of love.

"He (Christ) is wounded with love for the bride. The Bridegroom bears a great love for the solitude of the soul; but He is wounded much more by her love, since being wounded with love for Him, she desired to live alone in respect to all things. And He does not wish to leave her alone, but wounded by the solitude she embraces for His sake, and observing that she is dissatisfied with any other thing, He alone guides her, drawing her to and absorbing her in Himself. Had He not found her in spiritual solitude, He would not have wrought this in her." (p. 545)

"Strange it is, this property of lovers, that they like to enjoy one another's companionship alone, apart from every creature and all company. If some stranger is present, they do not enjoy each other freely. . . . The reason they desire to commune with each other alone is that love is a union between two alone." (p. 545)

A popular song of my youth put it humorously: "I want to get you on a slow boat to China, all to myself, alone. . . ." What is there in John's image of spiritual union which is so poignant and thrilling? Is it not that underneath all the layers of disillusioned cynicism each of us still longs for absolute fulfillment — to give and receive perfect love? We know that human beings can give such love only fleetingly. The kind that lasts is warm and tender, but rarely intense and exalting.

It is incredible to think that God could love us this way. Yet secretly, we do believe it is possible — if what we are speaking of is God's ability to give, and within ourselves, what the mystics call "the virgin point" or "the divine spark". From time to time do we recognize that there is a stream of pure, beautiful love inside us, waiting for its opportunity to flow?

But we also know just as deeply that we cannot actualize that reality amidst the tugs and pulls of daily life. To come into that mystery we would have to be alone — not only physically, but interiorly. And when, at privileged moments, we have experienced God reaching into that sacred place, afterwards we ponder on what we could do to extend that experience in some way. St. John of the Cross, St. Catherine of Siena, and all the mystics lived so securely centered in God that they brought Him with them everywhere, even down the highways and byways of ordinary life.

And that is where the terrible part of St. John's doctrine comes in again. He claims that the only way to enter permanent union with the God who can ravish our solitude with bliss is by means of asceticism.

His translator, Kieran Kavanaugh, summarizes one of the many of St. John's illustrations of the ascetical way as follows:

"God (compared to the sun) is ever present in the soul (compared to the window) communicating and preserving its natural being, just as the sun shines on the window.

"When the window is wholly smeared with dirt, the sun does not illumine it, as it does when the window is unstained; likewise a soul utterly smeared with inordinate affection for creatures is unprepared to receive the communication of God's supernatural being.

"In the measure that the window is clean, the sun illumines it; as the soul through love wipes away everything unconformed to the divine will, God communicates Himself supernaturally, or through grace.

"When the window is entirely clean, the sunlight so illumines it that it makes it appear to be the light. Yet, regardless of its total resemblance to the light, the window in its nature remains distinct from the nature of the sunlight. Similarly when the soul in its activity is completely purified of everything unlike God, when it is entirely conformed with God's will through love, God will so communicate His supernatural being that it will be like God and seem to be God. Yet in its nature it will be as distinct from God as before." (St. John of the Cross, *Collected Works*, p. 46)

This concept of asceticism is certainly no more frightening than that of Our Lord Himself, who says, "Be ye perfect." Jesus had but one desire: to do the will of the Father, by loving Him with His whole heart, mind and strength, and by loving those sent by the Father as He loved Himself. So, are we seeking an easier path than Jesus chose? Unfortunately, yes. I think what strikes fear into me when reading St. John is that I am always hoping to find, not the Cross, but a shortcut. Isn't there some way that I could drown in spiritual bliss and then peacefully overflow in love to everyone around me, without having to be painfully stripped of everything else? Yet, again and again, the answer comes, "Only he who loses himself can find himself." It is only when I accept the unchangeable crosses of life with a willing heart — when I offer myself unconditionally to Christ as His instrument, that the peaceful joy of being His can come to me. Otherwise I writhe on the cross, cursing my fate, pushing the nails in still further. As in the drawing of the Ascent of Mount Carmel, "In this nakedness the spirit finds its rest, for when it covets nothing, nothing raises it up, and nothing weighs it down, because it is in the center of its humility." (St John of the Cross, *Collected Works*, p. 67)

Some expressions used by St. John of the Cross in his descriptions of the ascent are a bit puzzling. He writes both of the dark night of the senses and the dark night of the soul. The lines in the poem are more romantic than the realities:

> One dark night,
> Fired with love's urgent longings
> — Ah, the sheer grace! — I went out unseen,
> My house being now all stilled.

St. John describes the dark night of the senses this way: "To undertake the journey to God the heart must be burned and purified of all creatures with the fire of divine love. Such a purgation puts the devil to flight, for he has power over a man attached to temporal and bodily things." (St. John of the Cross, *The Ascent of Mt. Carmel*, p. 75)

Such an ascetical flight from creatures means not only fasts and mortifications, though these are recommended, but more than that, means a detachment of the affections from everything besides God. We are allowed to love everything God has made ordinately, which means, according to its God-given place in our lives, but not with greedy abandon as if these things could fulfill us. To give my own examples: to eat a good meal with gratitude is Christian. To overeat is not only destructive to one's own body and soul but uncharitable to the poor. To love a friend as a wonderful gift of God is holy. To cling to a friend possessively in over-dependence is to put that friend in the place of Christ Himself, on whom alone we can depend for our salvation. St. Augustine is said to have written, "It is all right to love creatures but we shouldn't depend upon them."

The dark night of the senses consists in actively overcoming our disordered affections, but also consists in passively experiencing the limitations of all finite being. As God purifies our hearts, we find that a certain distaste for the things of the world replaces our desire for them. This can be quite painful. For a while it may seem as if everything has lost its savor . . . "vanity, all is vanity" . . . while the spiritual riches, which are to replace the worldly ones, are not yet clearly within our grasp.

The dark night of the senses is difficult, but still worse is the dark night of the soul. In this night, we must detach ourselves from our desire to hold onto immaterial gifts in order to provide the time and place for the visitations of grace. St. John sometimes refers to this simply as *faith*! In faith, we embrace God alone, rather than the experiences that are associated with coming to know God.

It is easy to see what John of the Cross had in mind if we consider people we have known who appear to be religious phonies. Such people may often be sincere in their intentions, but one senses that they are not really interested in God Himself, or Christianity, or the welfare of their neighbors, but only in their own spiritual highs, their own spiritual "experiences."

The doctrine of the dark night used to cause me much dismay because I thought St. John meant that we weren't allowed to rejoice at all in God or His gifts. Closer study reveals, however, that the saint was not referring to the experience of God's simple presence tenderly loving us, but rather to unusual visions and locutions. These could be genuine, he maintained, but since they can also be produced by our imagination or feigned by the Devil, they should not become the center of our life with God. Like Job, I should be able to pray, "even if He slay me yet shall I love Him", convinced that whatever trials I might go through, worldly or spiritual, they are nothing in comparison to the inner bond of love between myself and God, which will be fulfilled in eternity.

John of the Cross spent his life in search of the ultimate love and found completion in his death in 1591. He was canonized in 1726, and declared a Doctor of the Church by Pope Pius XI in 1926.

I append here a selection from John's poetry, for one could say that all of his wisdom lies herein. The following is from *The Ascent of Mount Carmel*, pp. 68-69.

A song of the soul's happiness in having passed through the dark night of faith, in nakedness and purgation, to union with its Beloved.

> One dark night,
> Fired with love's urgent longings
> — Ah, the sheer grace! —
> I went out unseen,
> My house being now all stilled;
>
> In darkness, and secure,
> By the secret ladder, disguised,
> — Ah, the sheer grace! —
> In darkness and concealment
> My house being now all stilled;
>
> On that glad night,
> In secret, for no one saw me,
> Nor did I look at anything,
> With no other light or guide
> Than the one that burned in my heart;

This guided me
More surely than the light of noon
To where He waited for me
— Him I knew so well —
In a place where no one else appeared.

O guiding night!
O night more lovely than the dawn!
O night that has united
The Lover with His beloved,
Transforming the beloved in her Lover.

Upon my flowering breast
Which I kept wholly for Him alone,
There He lay sleeping,
And I caressing Him
There in a breeze from the fanning cedars.

When the breeze blew from the turret
Parting His hair, He wounded my neck
With His gentle hand,
Suspending all my senses.

I abandoned and forgot myself,
Laying my face on my Beloved;
All things ceased; I went out from myself,
Leaving my cares
Forgotten among the lilies.

St. John of the Cross asserts that when we reach the summit of the spiritual marriage with Christ the sweetness of such union far outweighs everything we have been through to reach that point. It appears from his writings, although he never refers to his own experiences directly, that John himself came into the highest form of union so that, regardless of all exterior persecutions he underwent, he was able to sustain a radiant peace and joy of soul. Reading John of the Cross gives me great hope of reaching the same degree of union.

FOR PERSONAL REFLECTION

1. When have you experienced solitude most profoundly?
2. Have you ever tried to deny yourself of sensory pleasures? How did you fare in these attempts?
3. What kinds of mystical experiences do you distrust in others and in yourself?   Does that critical awareness keep you from opening yourself to grace?   Do you think you need to be purified of "spiritual gluttony" by a dark night of the soul?
4. What balance of contemplation and action would be good for you at this time in your life?
5. When you sense that God is trying to move you into new experiences of Him do you tend to flee or to respond freely?

ST. BERNADETTE of LOURDES
(1844-1879)

Mary Neill

I had not intended to choose Bernadette Soubirous for my next reflection on a woman saint — one more Frenchwoman, one more child religious prodigy, one more short suffering-filled life cut off before her forties (when, for most of us, as Jung thought, the deepest religious quest begins).

Yet, visiting Lourdes for the second time in my life in 1987, I am drawn to reflect on the mysterious energy that emanated from the visions (sixteen in all) of this peasant girl; visions which took place beginning February 11, 1858.

Led by the memory of what this fourteen-year-old said she saw and heard over a hundred years ago, thousands of pilgrims gather daily in the Pyrenees Mountains near the flowing River Gave, to touch this rounded rock, this tomb-womb cave, to bathe in the nearby waters, asking forgiveness, healing, mercy of the Great Mother of God under her title "Immaculate Conception" ("tainted nature's solitary boast") — believing that her invisible touch can lift the burden of the many sorrows, the river of sorrows which they bring with them.

In Lourdes the sick are visible everywhere — in wheelchairs, on stretchers — young, old, dying. Perhaps Lourdes is the only place in the world where the sick rule. They are given precedence and honor; they are the chosen ones, the special.

When I had first visited Lourdes fourteen years ago, I had been warned against its commercialism, the outrageous Catholic kitsch, the superstitious crowds from all the world over, the religion that was good business and miracle-mongering. I was prepared for all this, and I found it. I was not prepared for the beauty of the hills and rivers, the simplicity of the devotion, the acceptance and living of all the opposites in this mountain refuge — life, death; sickness, health; joy, sadness — the sacredness and humanness of this place.

And so on that first visit, I quieted my inner, skeptical theologian who is educated to repeat, "This is not God; this is not God; this is not God," and I became a pilgrim — confessing, bathing in the cold waters.

I asked for two gifts on this holy ground. Not because my faith was simple and strong, but because of the faith of those I saw kneeling before the shrine, kissing the rock; because of those who had carved in hundreds of stones on the church walls, "I thank you Mother for . . . I thank you . . . I thank you . . . I thank you."

I asked, through the faith of the frail and constantly shaking man whom I saw one evening at the grotto, bending with great difficulty to kiss the rock to honor the Mother who had given life, who had known suffering, who could dissolve with her waters the inner hardness and the stones to throw against God and life — those stones which congeal around prolonged suffering. I asked, was he cured? Perhaps not; but something in me was touched and healed by seeing his acceptance, his asking, his simplicity.

I was given, in time, the two gifts I sought. "Ask and you shall receive." The good news is, "Healing of heart and of body can happen." The bad news is, "Suffering is everywhere."

The soul and the body are a continuum. Take your body on pilgrimage to a distant place. Wash it, bend it, pray with it, change its postures, its rigidities and inflexibilities so that your soul may bend before the mystery of birth and death. So bending, one easier knows, "I am not God; I am not God." One perhaps easier agrees to the strange contract that life has made with death and suffering — the very limitations that the Creator Father had to make with the nothingness, the stuff of creation.

To add our assent to this contract with death is both work and grace. Annie Dillard's images help penetrate this mystery:

> That something is everywhere and always amiss is part of the very stuff of creation. It is as though each clay form had baked into it, fired into it, a blue streak of nonbeing, a shaded emptiness like a bubble that not only shapes its very structure but that also causes it to list and ultimately explode. We could have planned things more mercifully, perhaps, but our plan would never get off the drawing board until we agreed to the very compromising terms that are the only ones that being offers.
>
> The world has signed a pact with the devil; it had to. It is a covenant to which every thing, even every hydrogen atom, is bound. The terms are clear: if you want to live, you have to die; you cannot have mountains and creeks without space, and space is a beauty married to a blind man. The blind man is Freedom, or Time, and he does not go anywhere without his great dog Death. The world came into being with the signing of the contract. A scientist calls it the Second Law of Thermodynamics. A poet says, "The Force that through the green fuse drives the flower/Drives my green age." This is what we know. The rest is gravy. (Annie Dillard, *Pilgrim at Tinker Creek* [NY: Bantam Books, 1976], p. 184)

Finally, that first time at Lourdes, I could ask for healing through the faith of this peasant girl Bernadette who, when painfully dying of bone tuberculosis could pray:

> I thank you Jesus, for everything; for the graces of my life; also for my weakness and infirmity; my faults of character and disposition, my humiliations, my limitations . . . I thank you for all of these.

This Bernadette whose last words, with a powerful and strong voice from her wasted body were "J'aime" . . . I love. What kinds of ways must our souls go so that our last words, our comment on life can be "I love . . . " Let us trace the stepping stones of Bernadette's life to ponder the mystery of grace at work in her.

1. Bernadette is born, January, 1844, the eldest child of a poor miller, Francois Soubirous and his wife, Louise. She is nursed by her godmother in a nearby village of Bartres; through her sickly, asthmatic childhood she often returns to this village where she watches the sheep. There are eventually three more children who live with their parents in a one-room hovel. Their poverty is great; there is no opportunity for education or preparation for First Communion. Bernadette cannot comprehend her catechism — she is slow.

2. When she is fourteen (small and dark, she appears to be about ten years old), on February 11, 1858, while gathering wood with her sister and cousin, she sees a beautiful woman in a grotto called Massabielle. Here is her own description of the event:

> "The Thursday before Ash Wednesday, it was cold and the weather was threatening. After our dinner my mother told us that there was no more wood in the house and she was vexed. My sister Toinette and I, to please her, offered to go and pick up dry branches by the riverside. My mother said 'no' because

the weather was bad and we might be in danger of falling into the Gave. Jeanne Abadie, our neighbor and friend, who was looking after her little brother in our house and who wanted to come with us, took her brother back to his house and returned the next moment telling us that she had leave to come with us. My mother still hesitated, but seeing that there were three of us she let us go. We took first of all the road which leads to the cemetery, by the side of which wood is unloaded and where shavings can sometimes be found. That day we found nothing there. We came down by the side which leads near the Gave and, having arrived at Pont Vieux, we wondered if it would be best to go up or down the river. We decided to go down and, taking the forest road, we arrived at Merlasse. There we went into Monsieur de la Fitte's field by the mill of Savy. As soon as we had reached the end of this field, nearly opposite the grotto of Massabielle, we were stopped by the canal of the mill we had just passed. The current of this canal was not strong for the mill was not working, but the water was cold and I for my part was afraid to go in. Jeanne Abadie and my sister, less timid than I, took their sabots in their hand and crossed the stream. However, when they were on the other side, they called out that it was cold and bent down to rub their feet and warm them. All this increased my fear, and I thought that if I went into the water I should get an attack of asthma. So I asked Jeanne Abadie, who was bigger and stronger than I, to take me on her shoulders.

" 'I should think not,' answered Jeanne; 'you're a mollycoddle; if you won't come, stay where you are.'

"After the others had picked up some pieces of wood under the grotto they disappeared along the Gave. When I was alone I threw some stones into the bed of the river to give me a foothold, but it was of no use. So I had to make up my mind to take off my sabots and cross the canal as Jeanne and my sister had done.

"I had just begun to take off my first stocking when suddenly I heard a great noise like the sound of a storm. I looked to the right, to the left, under the trees of the river, but nothing moved; I thought I was mistaken. I went on taking off my shoes and stockings; then I heard a fresh noise like the first. I was frightened and stood straight up. I lost all power of speech and thought when, turning my head toward the grotto, I saw at one of the openings of the rock a rosebush, one only, moving as if it were very windy. Almost at the same time there came out of the interior of the grotto a golden-colored cloud, and soon after a Lady, young and beautiful, exceedingly beautiful, the like of whom I had never seen, came and placed herself at the entrance of the opening above the rosebush. She looked at me immediately, smiled at me and signed to me to advance, as if she had been my mother. All fear had left me but I seemed to know no longer where I was. I rubbed my eyes, I shut them, I opened them; but the Lady was still there continuing to smile at me and making me understand that I was not mistaken. Without thinking of what I was doing, I took my rosary in my hands and went on my knees. The Lady made a sign of approval with her head and herself took into her hands a rosary which hung on her right arm. When I attempted to begin the rosary and tried to lift my hand to my forehead, my arm remained paralyzed, and it was only after the Lady had signed herself that I could do the same. *The Lady left me to pray all alone; she passed the beads of her rosary between her fingers but she said nothing; only at the end of each decade did she say the 'Gloria' with me.*

"When the recitation of the rosary was finished, the Lady returned to the interior of the rock and the golden cloud disappeared with her.

"As soon as the Lady had disappeared Jeanne Abadie and my sister returned to the grotto and found me on my knees in the same place where they had left me. They laughed at me, called me imbecile and bigot, and asked me if I would go back with them or not. I had now no difficulty in going into the stream, and I felt the water as warm as the water for washing plates and dishes.

" 'You had no reason to make such an outcry,' I said to Jeanne and Marie while drying my feet; the water of the canal is not so cold as you seemed to make me believe!'

" 'You are very fortunate not to find it so; we found it very cold.'

"We bound up in three fagots the branches and fragments of wood which my companions had brought; then we climbed the slope of Massabielle and took the forest road. Whilst we were going toward the town I asked Jeanne and Marie if they had noticed anything at the grotto.

" 'No,' they answered, 'Why do you ask us?'

" 'Oh, nothing,' I replied indifferently.

"However, before we got to the house, I told my sister Marie of the extraordinary things which had happened to me at the grotto, asking her to keep it secret.

"Throughout the whole day the image of the Lady remained in my mind. In the evening at the family prayer I was troubled and began to cry.

" 'What is the matter?' asked my mother.

"Marie hastened to answer for me and I was obliged to give the account of the wonder which had come to me that day.

" 'These are illusions,' answered my mother; 'you must drive these ideas out of your head and especially not go back again to Massabielle.'

"We went to bed but I could not sleep. The face of the Lady, so good and so gracious, returned incessantly to my memory, and it was useless to recall what my mother had said to me; I could not believe that I had been deceived." (F.P. Keyes, *The Sublime Shepherdess*)

3. Though her mother berates her for "these illusions which no one else can see", Bernadette, feeling that she could not be deceived, returns to the grotto and washes her face in it; eats grass; asks the woman's name, and is finally told in her own dialect the woman's title, "Que soy era Immaculada councepsiou." Bernadette does not know what the words mean, though the doctrine of the Immaculate Conception had been declared an infallible teaching of the Church in 1854. She is told by the woman to go to the parish priest and ask that a chapel be built and that processions be made with candles to the place. In fear and trembling, Bernadette faces the Curé Peyrmale who does everything to fight these illusions of this illiterate, asthmatic, stubborn peasant girl.

4. From the beginning there are those who believe Bernadette and follow her in growing numbers to the rock near the River Gave. They watch her transparent face as she talks to the woman, "The most beautiful woman I have ever seen." They believe in the light "no bigger than I" that shines from the child's face, turned toward a face they cannot see. They bathe in the stream; a blind stonecutter is cured. The last apparition to Bernadette is on the feast of Our Lady of Carmel in July 1858. The crowds grow all the while, and the harassment of Bernadette begins.

5. The faithful harass her — touch this, touch that. The mayor harasses her; her family does not understand. Bernadette clings to her story, the memory of the voice and the visions. She cannot be moved. One has only to see the photographs of these tough-faced men to imagine the harshness they brought against this frail girl. She persists. The newspapers, even in Paris, speculate about the event. Zola writes about this "abnormal hysteria." The Emperor Napoleon III, influenced by his wife, orders the grotto opened. Thousands upon thousands come, bearing candles in procession as the beautiful woman asked. They come; many experience physical and mental healing. A great basilica is built in 1876.

6. Bernadette's simple life with her parents is changed. The family is moved to a better house which one may see today — the bed she slept in, the bed her mother died in, the fireplace. Many photographs of Bernadette are taken: "kneel" "sit" "fold your hands" "look at this statue". The photographs of her in her simple peasant costume show her strength and simplicity. She must tell her story over and over. Finally, she makes her First Communion. She becomes a boarder at the school conducted by the Sisters of Nevers and helps them with young children at the hospice they run in Lourdes. She is a slow learner. The Bishop feels that she should enter religious life, though she is not the usual fabric from which the Ladies of Nevers form their postulants. She obeys, fainting as she leaves her mother, her culture, the beloved grotto. She is homesick to the core at the novitiate in Nevers. (She sees a city for the first time enroute to Nevers.) When asked by the Mother Superior what she can do, she answers, "pas grand chose" (nothing much). "Perhaps grate carrots?" Her twelve years as a religious begin — her sturdy and simple peasant life gone. But she is much protected from the publicity and harassment of faithful and unfaithful alike.

7. The years in the convent are uneventful except for the moments when she is summoned to the parlor to tell some

eminent and curious visitors the story yet one more time. Often she weeps before entering the parlor, crying, "Why can't they leave me alone?" Though her health is not good, she works in the sacristy, then in the infirmary as a nurse during the Franco-Prussian War. Her stolid and quiet presence comforts the French soldiers who do not know who she is. This same simplicity is a source of irritation to her Superior who confessed afterwards that whenever she had occasion to address Bernadette, she found herself speaking with a certain harshness to this "crude and ignorant peasant" ("Une paysanne et sans instruction"). Bernadette's life is so uneventful that one authority writes:

> In all the annals of sanctity it would be hard to find the counterpart of the history of Bernadette Soubirous, for she did nothing out of the common, she said nothing memorable; she gathered no followers around her, she had in the ordinary sense no revelations, she did not prophesy or read men's thoughts; she was remarkable for no great austerities or striking renunciations or marvelous observance of rule or conspicuous zeal for souls. . . . (Frank Sheed, *Saints Are Not Sad*, p. 423)

8. Bernadette is particularly kind to newly arrived novices, remembering her own homesickness and the heart-rending farewell she had bidden to her land and her people. When asked how to meditate, she says, "I cannot meditate." Though humble before humiliations, she can be sharp-tongued with fools. When one man says, "The Lady had better teach you how to speak correct French," Bernadette replies, "At least she did not teach me to laugh at ignorant people." From first to last, she was just herself. She knew that she was ignorant, inexperienced, altogether undeserving of the high favors granted to her.

9. Her death from bone tuberculosis is long and painful. She cries out in pain; she asks for narcotics, and grows frightened of the dark and of shadows on the wall of her bedroom. She makes no effort to die "heroically" — to appear as a saint. When, shortly before her death, she is asked once more to recount the story of the apparitions by those who had heard rumors of her disquieting dying, she sobs convulsively after the interrogation though the Mother Superior assures her this will be the last time. "Oh, you don't know," Bernadette cries. The interrogation is a bitter reminder of the thousands of questions she answered earlier, never wavering in her account. "This is what I have seen. I am not obliged to make you believe it." The problem for the authorities remains that she is the sole (and unworthy) witness to this vision. Bernadette is not surprised by her unworthiness; they are.

10. She dies in Holy Week, propped up in an armchair. She holds a crucifix, kisses it, asks for a drink of water, cries out, "I love . . ." and dies as those at her bedside pray, "Holy Mary, Mother of God, pray for us sinners now and at the hour of our death." Her body, incorrupt when exhumed, lies exposed in a glass casket in Nevers, defenseless still against the curious onlookers.

There is something that disturbs me about Bernadette, just as she was disconcerting to those in her lifetime. I am not sure if I am disturbed by my sophisticated sinfulness which is illuminated by her intense simplicity, or if my resistance is, not to her sanctity, but to the cultural setting which makes it difficult for me to feed upon the heart of her great gift. What are the unessentials that can be pushed aside so that the inexplicable core can shine? If she is my sister, how can I reach her across the vast distances that stretch between us? From her, am I to learn to distrust my learning? To trust every reported apparition of the great Mother? To imitate her refusal to ask to be healed? Her acceptance of the Lady's statement that earth was not to be a place of happiness for her? To let myself be used not just by God's inner revelations to me, but by the religious structures, the Church?

What are you asking of me, Sister Bernadette? What do you mean to me? What are you telling me? That I think it is wrong not to ask for healing? That I feel that although the great Mother may appear in distant places amidst fanfare and crowds, she is better sought inwardly in quiet, gentle, less spectacular ways? If I were Jesus, I would let my mother rest and not have her working continually overtime, appearing now at this shrine, now at that. Christ once for all entered into the temple and purchased us by His blood — I feel that Mary once and for all in her life showed us the fierce and healing waters of the feminine way. I believe that God is at least as kind as I am, and that if so, I would want those I love to experience profoundly and often, the beauty and happiness and grandeur of life on earth (what is found now is found then) and not demand of them a daily grinding of pain, of inordinate suffering. Love needs to be annealed in the fire of great suffering, yes; but it needs also the quiet and gentle and banal days of simply being together. Where am I right in these opinions, where am I wrong? What do you tell me to do, Bernadette?

I hear her say to me:

"A way is just a way. I obeyed because it was the way given me; shown me. My way was simple because I was. When they tried to make me embellish the story, I could not. I embroidered only on cloth. I could only be true to my limits and so then true to the limits of all who surrounded me — my loving but careless parents; the harsh and limited Curé; the skeptical mayor; the pushy crowds; the severe nuns; the mottled Church. The core of my belief was that the most

beautiful woman of all, so kind and loving, looked at me,
talked to me, accepted and loved me. She was 'a girl no bigger
than I,' and I knew in my heart that if she accepted me, I could
not be deceived."

Bernadette says to me:

"Mary, you are always pushing boundaries, testing limits —
that is not the feminine way — to be spirit which encompasses all the hard angles. You push your limits; you push the
Church's limits. It is, like you and me, just a group of
convicted sinners, at its best. You are still haunted by the
masculine sternness and disciplined ideal of the Port Royal
French spirituality which stressed always one's own will. You
cannot will yourself to heaven, to love, to perfection. My
sturdiness was that as a French peasant, I was protected
against the charms of that French spirituality which lingers in
you and in the Church. I am just a *paysanne grossiere*; you have
strong peasant blood in you, too — but you don't want the
spiritual elite to look down on you. I just couldn't be other
than I was, once the Lady looked down on me. A shepherdess
close to the earth, living in dirt as a child, grounded in the hills
around Lourdes, I kept close to the earth and let heaven's light
come down to me. I was no climber, no pretender. I didn't
want to be a Bernadette that God had never heard of. Don't
try to be a Mary that God has never heard of. It is only the
heavenly Mother who with her gaze of unconditional love can
help you believe that this is God's judgment on you now,
despite all your confusion and cowardice: unconditional love,
just as you are. You are enough. He is enough. Little and poor
and ignorant as I was, I was enough. Let be. Thank God for
your limitations — they are His love, also."

FOR PERSONAL REFLECTION

1. Have you ever made a pilgrimage, inner or outer? What change was wrought in you because of this?
2. Have you ever refused to ask God to take a suffering from you? Describe the suffering, the experience of prayer.
3. To what degree do you labor under the burden of perfectionism? Voluntarism? (through will-power you can become a saint)
4. Vividly imagine the Blessed Virgin appearing to you. Where are you? What does she wear? What does she say? Who is with you? Do a dialogue with her about the meaning of the many public apparitions. Do you find it hard or easy to believe that Jesus' Mother appears in our times?
5. It was the face of Bernadette that struck those who saw her during the apparitions. When have you ever been struck by the radiance in another's face?
6. The radiant woman told Bernadette that she was the Immaculate Conception. This doctrine, this mystery says something about lightness, pure lightness coming from darkness; about generation and conception; about naming some new mystery of being, that the twentieth century needs to hear. What are titles of Our Lady that you find easier to relate to? What for you, is the inner meaning, the possible connection you can make to the Immaculate Conception?
7. What are the qualities of Bernadette which you like? Dislike? Write a dialogue with her — what does she say to you?

ST. THERESE of LISIEUX (1873-1897)

Mary Neill

"The holy," says Rudolph Otto, is always *"facinans tremendum,"* both fascinating and fearful. Attractive and repulsive. No saint more embodies this quality of the holy, for me, than Therese of Lisieux.

As a freshman in high school, one afternoon I took home the library copy of her autobiography, *The Story of A Soul,* and read it in one sitting. When I finished, I sat in a bathtub full of water and sobbed and sobbed. How to account for the power of that slim volume on someone far removed in time and culture? It was this same account of her life, sent to various Carmelite convents after her death which spread the devotion to Therese that resulted in her canonization in 1927, 54 years after she was *born.* Thirteen years after they had published 2000 copies of her autobiography, the Carmelite convent where she died was receiving 5000 letters *a day.*

There has been no cult in modern times to equal that of Therese; there has been no saint so early canonized; no saint canonized who did, like she, only little things; no saint canonized whose Way has been authenticated by the Church as valid. Joan of Arc was burned at the stake and waited 500 years to be canonized and be named patron of France. Francis Xavier traveled thousands of miles, preached the gospel incessantly, died a martyr and so was named patron of missions. Therese, entering the convent at fourteen and dying at twenty-four, was also made by the Church patron of France, equal to Joan of Arc, and equal patron with Francis Xavier of the missions. Incredible.

Could it be that in canonizing her the Church was calling attention to the inner journey, to the "emigres de l'Interieur" who experience other martyrdoms and dangerous adventures? "We have all of Africa and Asia within us," wrote Thomas Wolfe. Therese traversed the inner geography of the soul in some profound way to which many, who read her life, feel a kinship. She found her way through the thickets, despite all obstacles, inner and outer (one of which was, as she herself admitted, "I never grew up"). She gives us courage to make that inner journey, to find the way that is true to our lives.

As I try to remember why I cried after reading her auto-biography, I think now it was for the wrong reasons. I saw instantly how much she loved God and was loved by Him. I felt cheated. I was jealous of her pious family, her heavily Catholic culture, the obsession with religious life that both parents and all her sisters had. No wonder she was a saint — her whole life was filled with rituals and God-talk and religious culture. She had a head start. I was born in the wrong time and place and culture ever to become a saint. This wasn't fair. Now I see that I had missed the point. I thought her power came from the culture rather than from transcending it.

Recently re-reading many books about Therese, I found myself appalled by what I had once thought her essential good luck — that "closed room 19th century Catholic culture" that jumps from the pages of her story with its hatred of the body, fear of friendship, childish baby talk, contempt for the world, preoccupation with death and the future life — its narrowness and radical distaste for joy. I quote a few passages to illustrate the point and remind myself why Pope John XXIII thought some windows of the Church ought to be opened by the Second Vatican Council. She writes:

> I have always noticed that I have a great capacity for suffering and very little for rejoicing. Joy seems to take away my taste for food, whereas on the days I have much to suffer, I have a ravenous appetite. It is a fact that my system cannot take too much joy. I shall always be grateful to Our Lord for turning early friendships into bitterness for me, because with a nature like mine, I could so easily have fallen into a snare and had my wings clipped. (St. Therese of Lisieux, *The Story of A Soul*, p. 113)

She prayed that her sister would not enjoy a dance she was invited to. She was thrilled when her sister left the dance sick. Therese considered that God had answered her prayers.

But enough. It is easy to find what is limiting and neurotic about Therese. It is fascinating to wonder how she found her way to be connected to God, in season and out, in such a way that the power of His love flowed to others in her life, in her agonizing death (she took two months to die, inch by inch) and after her death. Ida Goerres in *The Hidden Face* describes how Therese's writings, conversation and life bore this out:

> The root of them all was the same, the same root from which Therese in childhood had derived strength during all serious crises: her loyalty toward her conscience at all costs, and her obedience, which was the garb of this loyalty. Ruthlessly Therese transcended her own state of mind and her own feelings. She knew what was true and real whether or not she felt, understood or experienced it. The Sun *was* in the sky, even if she were blinded. She had seen the radiant light; she knew she had seen it; and even if she no longer knew — it had

vanished to such remote spaces — she still knew that she had
known it once, and that would have to satisfy her. And so she
wrote and prayed as if nothing had happened, as if her whole
inner world had not been buried by an earthquake. (Goerres,
p. 360)

She was enlightened; even in the dark she did not deny the
light. If you see photographs of her (the originals, not those
touched up to prettify her face) you see her power and her pain.
She did not squander her pain. How did she find this direction
(she who was to say that many more souls could find sanctity if
they had good direction)?

Until her mother died, when Therese was four and a half,
she experienced a childhood of unconditional love that few
experience.

A happy childhood means above all a loved child. . . . Because
she was a loved child, she received from the beginning the
knowledge . . . *that we can be loved without having deserved it*:
that grace comes first. . . . It is bliss simply to be someone's
child, child of a father, of a mother, living, moving and having
its being in a love which is unmerited, unmeritable, anticipat-
ory, unconditional and immutable. (Goerres, p. 42)

After her mother's death, the next years of Therese's life
were ones of separation and torment. An older sister would
mother her and then leave her to enter the convent — and then
another. She became shy, oversensitive, scrupulous, an outsider
and an eccentric. She was taken out of school. She became
seriously ill. Her early childhood Garden of Eden had become a
garden of agony. In May when she was ten years old, she
experienced a miraculous cure of illness — she cried "Mama,
Mama" to the Virgin's statue and experienced healing.

Christmas of the same year she had what she called her "second conversion" — an ability to control her hypersensitive feelings.

Once she had believed and obeyed the grace of her conversion, she never looked back in her commitment to return God's unconditional love, whether she experienced His will as sweet as when she was cossetted as a child, or hard, as when she spent years in spiritual dryness at prayer, or very hard as when she lay dying.

> The very desires and intuitions of my inmost heart assured me that another and more lovely land awaited me, an abiding city. . . . Then suddenly the fog about me seems to enter my very soul, and fill it to such an extent that I cannot even find there the lovely picture I had formed of my homeland; everything had disappeared.
>
> To Pauline Therese had said earlier: "Be very careful, when you have to care for such patients again, never to leave poisonous medicines standing by their bedside. I assure you, it takes only a moment to lose one's control when one has such pain." (Goerres, pp. 374-375)

Yet, despite this agonizing, slow death, she never ceased to love her God, her life, her sisters, herself unconditionally.

> I expect you will think I am rather exaggerating the night of my soul; to judge by the poems I have written this year, I must appear to be overwhelmed with consolation, a child for whom the veil of faith is almost torn apart; yet it is no longer a veil — it is a wall reaching almost to Heaven, shutting out the stars. When I sing of Heaven's happiness, of what it is to possess God forever, I feel no joy; I simply sing *of what I want to believe.* (Goerres, p. 357)

How we whimper and whine in our sufferings and darkness; how we fail to love God unconditionally, to love as He does — in season and out. How we hate our wounds — we are so unlike Therese who prayed: "The only grace I ask for is that it shall be a wounded life, wounded by love." How purely she willed one thing: to launch herself toward God with a cry of grateful love, "Whether from the crest of joy or the trough of despair."

As a child her earthly father had shown her that her name was written in Heaven (The "T" made by the belt of Orion). She had believed and followed. "In the end, if we are to trust anything at all, we have to trust what was given us." Therese trusted and followed early on what was given her.

It is only after some years of studying Eastern religions that I can see more clearly the profundity of Therese's spiritual insight and certitude. The Taoists had written thousands of years ago: "Mature virtue is perfected in the spirit of childhood" (Lao-tsu) and "The great man is he who has not lost the heart of a child." (Mencius)

Therese found in reading the gospels and in the infirmities of her own life and temperament the way she must go. Because she was weak, like the Holy Innocents and the Good Thief, she would have to steal heaven. She found her nearness to God not in fullness of righteousness, but in the receptive emptiness of her poverty.

With amazing wisdom she tells Celine: "Do not try to rise above your trials, for we are too small to rise above our difficulties. Therefore let us try to pass under them." At sixteen she writes: "If you bear in peace the trial of being displeasing to yourself, you offer a sweet shelter to Jesus. It is true that it hurts you to find yourself thrust outside the door of your own self, so to speak, but fear not; the poorer you become, the more Jesus will love you."

She was seized and marked by God's holiness because she seized and used everything as a fulcrum to Him — we cast about waiting for the right experience or scene or person or book to deliver us. We read many books; she read only a few, especially the *Imitation of Christ* and the New Testament — moreover, she lived them. We choose to love lovable people; she loved those who were given her. We hate our neuroses, our abandonments; she turned hers over to God. We seek to be public and interesting; she sought to be hidden and uninteresting. We seek understanding; she did not seek to be understood. She practiced concealment (as lovers do); we show ourselves off. We want our way, but we do not find the way to our purest possibility. We want to do great works; she prayed, "At the close of this life, I shall appear before Thee with empty hands, for I do not ask Thee, Lord, to count my works."

In his biography, *Storm of Glory*, John Beever imagines her saying:

> I am nobody. I did nothing great. Much of my life was spent
> in the laundry, in cleaning rooms, in looking after linen, in all
> the humdrum tasks of community life. I am not learned. I
> read very few books. I was neither poor nor rich. I was a little
> soul, an ordinary soul. But I loved God, and every work and
> act of mine was spoken and done with Him in complete
> possession of my heart. And that is all that counts. Nothing
> else is of the slightest value. (p. 263)

And I imagine her saying to us, as she did to her novices: "And you can do it too." She gives us her recipe for victory: "Run away."

In Therese as in no other saint, we have the journal of a soul which exposes her vulnerability and her beauty. The exposed soul evokes love, and makes one want to love. She did not hasten to tell her story, expose her troubles; she was reluctant. In the end, she exposed it in her journal only because of obedience. In her I see a deeply feminine way — the way the Taoists call the way of water — it yields, yet is strong, wears away stone through its movement. It conforms to any container — it follows its nature. Therese followed her nature and grew strong in love in doing so.

There is a way to read Therese's life that is maternal, observing the details of her external obedience — and missing the point of her internal obedience. Conformity is ever the enemy of spirituality and religion. I confuse inner and outer; I seek the security of conformity. The desire to be admired and noticed as "religious" by others may be the "give away" to a second-hand religious life. A life of sterility, lacking joy, peace, patience, self-control, kindness and all the other gifts is another "give away." "Hypocrisy is the deference that vice pays to virtue," Montaigne wrote. And we do little honor to Therese by mistaking the culture's feminine yielding for the inner spiritual yielding which every man and woman must make to his or her own God.

I love Therese because of her courage and honesty; her challenge to me to love God unconditionally; her strength against surface confirmation of her being; her acceptance of neurosis; her spontaneity. She never ceases to say something that surpasses me; to be someone that surprises me. She encompasses the opposites and is whole; she lived a short, hard life, unhonored, and now lives on in memory and works long and sweet and honorably. A child and yet a strong woman, hidden and yet open, determined to believe, yet honest about her doubts — a woman for our times, to remind us of the deep strength of the inner feminine.

I end, not with a prayer to her, but with one of her prayers, asking God for a loan of His love, as I would ask Therese to lend me her courage, her faith, her love. This is surely the comfort of the communion of saints:

My God you know the only thing I've ever wanted is to love you; I have no ambition for any other glory except that. In my childhood your love was waiting for me; as I grew up, it grew with me; and now it is like a great chasm whose depths are past sounding. Love breeds love; and mine, Jesus for you, keeps on thrusting out towards you as if to fill up that chasm which your love has made — but it's no good; mine is something less than a drop of dew lost in the ocean. Love you as you love me? The only way to do that is to come to you for the loan of your own love. I could not content myself with less.

FOR PERSONAL REFLECTION

1. What was your experience of unconditional love as a child? When have you ever experienced unconditional love? Given unconditional love?

2. When in your life have you sought to rid yourself of hypersensitivity?

3. When have you ever, like Therese, experienced spiritual dryness, yet made a determination to believe?

4. "In the end, if we are to trust anything at all, we have to trust what was given us." What from your familial and religious and educational background do you trust? What do you find difficult to trust?

5. To what extent are you plagued by the desire to be public and interesting? Have you ever met anyone who sought, like Therese, to be hidden and uninteresting?

6. Which of Therese's qualities do you most need "loaned to you"? Which of her qualities would you like to rid yourself of?

7. Imagine that you are asked to describe your *Way* to union with God.   What would it be?   What are your 10 commandments for spiritual growth?

8. Write a prayer to Therese or do dialogue with her asking her for spiritual direction.

ST. ELIZABETH SETON (1774-1821)

Ronda Chervin

I have saved St. Elizabeth Seton for the last. She is the saint for my family life and a sort of nemesis, for she has all the virtues I lack: patience, sweetness, prudence. An American, wife of a businessman, mother of five, teacher, and finally a sister and foundress of an order, there is none of the romantic European flavor of St. Catherine or St. Teresa in Elizabeth, nor any dramatic ecstasies to enable me to escape from the immediate implications of her witness in relationship to my own family duties.

I first read about St. Elizabeth Seton long before her recent canonization. The biography through which I met her originally (*Elizabeth Seton: An American Woman*, by Leonard Feeney, SJ) was surely written with the idea of the future canonization of the heroine in mind. Since then I have read many shorter accounts of her life, but none as enthusiastic and compelling as Fr. Feeney's, and so I will base my chapter on his version of her story.

Elizabeth Seton's own writings are to be found in collections of letters. Unfortunately the most interesting group is out of print and slowly crumbling to dust in the New York Public Library. Those letters I was able to obtain on inter-library loan, however, are even more apt to my purpose. For most of

Elizabeth's adult life she kept up a steady correspondence with her favorite childhood girlfriend. Such woman-to-woman correspondence gives a most vivid picture of the joys and trials of family existence and I will be quoting from the *Letters of Mother Seton to Mrs. Julianna Scott*, to illustrate Elizabeth Seton's approach to Christian life.

Born in New York City in 1774, the daughter of an excellent and extremely humane doctor of the Episcopalian upper classes, related to the Roosevelts, Elizabeth Bayley was much sought after. She was intelligent, charming, and beautiful.

All these natural virtues served to hide from others the spiritual struggles that were going on within this unusually pious young woman. So much did the contradictions and follies of ordinary life distress her, that by eighteen she considered suicide.

At that time, and throughout her life, it was compassion for others which drew her away from despairing thoughts. Elizabeth's father was put in charge of the care of the Irish immigrants who were flooding the country at that time, and who were left in quarantine outside the city. Elizabeth loved to help her father with his work. Of the sweet and outwardly serene disposition which Fr. Feeney considers typical of those saints who were always good, as compared to the great sinners become saints, Elizabeth was always a great comfort to those she nursed, both strangers and those within her own family.

Religiously, she was of the disposition of the "high" Anglicans, wearing a crucifix, bowing her head when the name of Jesus was spoken, keen on mortification, solitude and examinations of conscience. When quite young she was married to William Seton, a businessman of her set, involved with importing goods. There was much delighted love between the two in spite of the tremendous difficulties they began to face due to the collapse of William's financial affairs and his chronic ill-health, which eventually led to an early death.

Five children were born within eight years. Elizabeth was very maternal. She loved breast-feeding her babies. She was of a very merry temperament and enjoyed her children immensely.

And yet, in a letter to her friend Julianna, who had been widowed and was debating the advantages and disadvantages of remarriage, Elizabeth wrote that even in the best of unions the problems caused by differences of character far outweighed the joys!

Such an attitude characterized Elizabeth's entire approach to life. Sensitive and even ethereal of spirit, she found the inevitable annoyances of life in the world to be almost unendurable. But accepting these features as part of God's will for us on earth, she always did her best to ameliorate crosses, little or huge, by bringing love and humor into every situation.

Here is where she is so different from myself, and where she has so much to teach me. Of an ebullient temperament in youth, once faced with the challenges of adulthood, I fell into deep melancholy. Finding the Faith has given me a source of strength and hope, and yet the buoyancy to enjoy life for what it can give still eludes me. I pray that I may grow into such a renewal of youthfulness as "the child within" is healed.

All during her marriage and early motherhood, Elizabeth, while outwardly conforming to the patterns of her high-society environment, inwardly was developing an intense spiritual life. The fruits of prayer were manifest during the birth of her third child which almost cost her life, yet she did not fear to conceive twice more.

How dramatic was the manner in which she endured one of the heaviest times of her life: the illness and death of her beloved husband. Both husband and wife were exhausted from the extra work entailed by the gradual bankruptcy of the Seton business. Without funds to hire assistants, it was Elizabeth who would sit up late into the night doing the bookkeeping, after a day of tending the five children, and managing the home. As her husband's health waned, it was considered desirable to travel for a change of air to Italy, where the Setons had close business ties.

Taking her oldest daughter with her, they set sail for Leghorn (called in Italian, Livorno), the port city near Genoa. After a terrifying journey with William on the verge of death, they arrived only to be quarantined immediately in a cold damp hostel. Day and night, Elizabeth knelt by the cot of her husband praying aloud, and trying to bring him into the trustful state of grace she thought necessary to ensure his salvation.

During these last days of William's life Elizabeth never complained. Instead, she did her best to be gracious and loving to the Italian guards, posted to prevent possibly plague-stricken tourists from escaping and infecting the city. She tried to make their cell into the best home she could. One of my favorite images is of Elizabeth taking time when her dying husband was asleep, not to rest herself, but instead to skip rope with her lonely little daughter.

This touch seems to me so feminine and homey. Paul and Silas prayed in the stocks of their prison, but I cannot imagine them playing games. Elizabeth, however, was always, even later as a teaching nun, first of all *mother*. Never did she sink into self-pity. Always she overcame despair for the sake of the needs of those surrounding her.

Again, the contrast to my own behavior is striking. I, too, had a chronically ill husband who is now almost well, thank God. I recall that at the worst times of acute asthmatic attacks, what increased my anxiety no end was the presence of my fun-loving twins who, not understanding the danger of their father's condition, would jump on top of him, squeezing him around the neck when he could hardly breathe. Unable to laugh, I would shoo them away in anger. True, like Elizabeth, I would pray constantly, but this in such a state of panic that I doubt seriously if the sight of my pale face, lips moving spasmodically in supplication, would be much immediate comfort to my husband on the many unforgettable long night drives to the hospital.

But, perhaps, instead of berating myself for my lack of trust in Providence at times of anguish and fear, I should instead praise the Lord that we have survived that time. My imperfect prayers did bring down the graces to get through it all. My husband is now much better, and that, certainly due to healing graces.

In those years we had a little Elizabeth Seton joke. I told my daughters all about her, especially emphasizing her patience. So we devised a code-word they could use to stop me whenever I was being particularly irritated with them. In the midst of the fray a little girl would whisper in my ear, "Seton" — and then I would laugh and make an effort to calm down.

What was St. Elizabeth's secret? Complete trust in providence. As she told the guards, "If I had thought our condition the providence of man I would tear down your Lazaretto (quarantine clinic)." Instead, she regarded this dank cell as a sort of sacred home, for it was during this time that their marital union reached its peak as her husband was brought into complete surrender to God's will, sheltered in her loving arms. After thirty days, they were allowed to leave and move to the more comfortable home of his dear Italian Catholic business friends.

Just before his death, William begged for the last sacrament. There not being any Anglican Church in the vicinity, Elizabeth made up a service of her own. She was kneeling by his bed when he dreamed of Jesus. By previous agreement, at the moment of his death he squeezed the hand of his dear wife for the last time to signify that he was at peace with the Lord.

Here begins one of the most interesting periods of the life of our saint. The friends, in whose home her husband died, were devout "daily Mass" Catholics. Accompanying them to services, Elizabeth began to feel moved toward the Blessed Sacrament and toward Mary. At the same time that she was drawn closer and closer to the Catholic religion, she also came into a deep spiritual friendship with her married host. This love, which grew throughout the years sparkled by correspondence and very infrequent visits from Italy to America, where Elizabeth returned shortly afterwards, was to sustain her not only in her conversion but also in the development of the intense religious life she was to follow in later years.

The return of Elizabeth and her daughter to New York City ushered in a time of many sufferings. First of all, they found themselves paupers. They received some help from relatives but basically the Setons were reduced from an upper-class mode of living to the most meager circumstances.

It is delightful to read, in her biography and in her letters, how joyfully Elizabeth adjusted to this change. Inwardly, she had always intensely disliked the fuss and phoniness involved in society life. In spite of the enormous burden of household work, she was quite pleased to be free of much of the outside world and to devote herself to her children. To distract them from their melancholy feelings, after losing their father, she would spend hours playing with them, devising ingenious games, involving them in music and dance.

Gradually, she began to consider conversion to Catholicism. Her decision to be received in the Catholic Church was fraught with difficulties. She has taken a small job working as schoolmistress in an Anglican school. Would they keep her on if she became a Catholic? She needed the money desperately. Almost every member of her husband's family was appalled that she would consider such a change — so great was the prejudice against the Catholic Church. They were especially upset because they saw that Elizabeth had began to influence several of the other young women of the family toward the same decision.

As Fr. Feeney point out, "there must be an intense personal realization of the mysteries of Christianity before the miseries of it can be supported." (Feeney, p. 20) It was Elizabeth's conviction of the truths of the Faith, coming through prayer as well as from the influence of her Italian friends, that brought her to fling herself into so unpopular a decision, regardless of the consequences. She was never to regret this decision and her sense of the presence of Christ in the Church was to grow continually.

As a convert myself, who had to endure quite a bit, I can relate to the unhappy consequences of her conversion which were not long in coming. Elizabeth endured much persecution from the family, and still greater poverty. She was able to survive because of the help of her own family, her Italian friends, and that of her great friend Julianna, who sent her a small sum of money every month. All the while, Elizabeth Seton nurtured a dream about the role she might play in the Church. She loved children, she loved learning, she loved the poor, and she loved the Lord. Why couldn't she found a Catholic school as good as the existing Episcopalian schools, not for the rich, but for the poor?

Yet, how could she, a poor woman with five children to raise, bring such a plan to fruition? After many difficulties, Elizabeth opened a very small school at Emmitsburg, Maryland. She was given a special dispensation to take religious vows with a proviso that she would put the interests of her children before any religious duties. The older boys were sent to a school connected with the Seminary and the younger girls were allowed to stay with her and participate in the life of the school. So began her order, the Sisters of Charity, which is still flourishing today.

As shown in the film about Mother Seton's life, made to celebrate her canonization, this school was extremely poor and was integrated — quite a feat in those times. In spite of the hard physical labor required to keep the school running, the spirit was always merry, catching fire from Mother Seton herself.

Such good cheer was by no means a result of a change in the Seton family fortunes. Our saint was pursued by Sister Death.

First came the early death of a sister-in-law who had converted and come to Maryland to be close to her beloved relative and spiritual guide, Elizabeth. Then came the deaths of her darling daughters, one after the other. These tragic events are powerfully described in the letters of the saint to her friend Julianna. Here are some of her own words about death and eternity:

"What can I say? They are both far dearer to me than myself. We part, nature groans, for me it is an anguish that threatens dissolution, not in convulsive sobs, but the soul is aghast, petrified. After ten minutes it returns to its usual motion, and all goes on as if nothing had happened. This same effect has followed the death of all so dear. Why? Faith lifts the staggering soul on one side, hope supports it on the other. Experience says it must be, and Love says — let it be." (*Letters*, p. 197)

Here is a very feminine image of the same response to death:

"I am sending my rose-buds to bloom in heaven. You, (Julianna) looking over the sharp thorns which will grow on the rising stem, think more of the sweet odor they exhale in your own bosom. Ungenerous, selfish little mother, when will you grow wise? The long, long look through the clouds, and it (my soul) cries to Him who loves to read what is unutterable. . . . I can jump over all the troubles of this life with more gaiety and real lightness of heart than ever . . . sometimes I can hardly contain my interior cheerfulness . . . and never so full of it as when I see these dear souls out of the world." (*Letters*, pp. 202ff)

How could a mother write such a thing unless in prayer? She had come so close to Jesus and Mary she could feel her loved ones safe in their heavenly home!

About the death of loved ones she advises: "Let the hand (God's) which gave the blow heal it." (*Letters*, p. 22)

One of her daughters when on her deathbed confided to her sisters, "Oh, be sure always to pray in earnest. For in the end you will have to leave this earth and dear Mommy will not be able to go with you."

Indeed Elizabeth frequently lamented the horror of death for those unprepared. "The soul departing without hope; its views, its interests centered in a world it is hurried from. No father's sheltering arms, no heavenly home of joy. Eternity — a word of transport, or of agony. Your friend, your own, your true, your dear friend, begs you, supplicates you, in the name of God — think of it. Oh! If she (Elizabeth) should see your (Julianna's) precious soul torn, dragged away an unwilling victim — what a thought of horror!" (*Letters*, p. 146)

Her own death came not far behind, and she greeted it quite in character. "Eternity, eternity, when shall I come to you at last?" Her dying word was: "Jesus."

In one of her last letters to her life-long friend she devises this charming analogy in an attempt to convince her to join her in becoming a Catholic.

"Peace, my dear . . . we will jog up the hill as quietly as possible, and when the flies and mosquitos bite, wrap the cloak round and never mind them; they can only penetrate the surface. Darling Julia, how I wish you would have such a Catholic cloak also."

Dear Mother Seton, if you were my next door neighbor what would you tell me day by day about how to be a holy wife and mother? Well, you are in eternity, not in Los Angeles. But in the Spirit all things are possible. Won't you come into my heart and be my best friend? Tell me what you would do. Cajole me into laughing a little more. Show me how to love my husband, my daughters, my son, with the love they deserve and need. Amen.

This evening my eleven-year-old son walked by and said "Mommy, I'm so glad I have you and Daddy for parents. Some parents don't even care about their kids. And you've given me the consolation of God. Without you I'd never have any consolation in the whole world."

FOR PERSONAL REFLECTION

1. When you meet patient, sweet women do you identify with them or does it cause in you envy and resentment?
2. Are there situations in your own life now which could use sweetness and patience?   If so, what thoughts and feelings toward others help you to become kinder toward them?
3. Does helping others bring you out of despair?   If so, what works might you undertake which require compassionate care?
4. How do you react to the illness of others?   How do you respond to death?   What prayerful exercises might you devise to bring you deeper into this mystery?
5. Have you ever had to choose between God and human love?   God's will and your own security in the world?   How have your choices affected your life?
6. Do you have dreams about possible ways you could serve the Church?   Do you have the courage to write out your plans and boldly try every means to put them into effect?
7. What are your images of eternity?   How would you convey them to the dying?
8. Write a dialogue with Elizabeth Seton letting her give you ideas about how to be a better wife, mother, teacher or friend.
9. What is your "cloak" that consoles, warms, and protects you?

Last Thoughts

Ronda Chervin

It has been said that the only criterion for becoming a saint is wanting to be one. And so, as the end of this exploration, I ask myself "Do I really want to be a saint?"

It seems to me that this question is being addressed to me by Christ over and over again — He shows me the vista of *infinite* love, *eternal* love, which He offers, and then I say Yes. He shows me the *infinite* pain, not eternal, which I will undergo as His intimate, and then I don't exactly say No, but my Yes becomes fainter and I withdraw slightly from the closeness of the embrace.

My Jesus, I want to be all Yes. Draw me beyond all human protectiveness into the mystery of being all yours. You have shown my heart the reasons, now, like the saints I admire so much, let me surrender.

Bibliography

Asch, Sholem. *The Apostle*. Translated by Maurice Samuel (New York: G.P. Putnam's Sons, 1943)

Bolt, Robert. *A Man for All Seasons* (New York: Random House, 1962)

Catherine of Siena. *The Dialogue*. Translated by Suzanne Noffke, O.P. (New Jersey: Paulist Press, 1980)

Farrow, John. *The Story of Thomas More* (New York: Sheed and Ward, 1954)

Feeney, Leonard. *Elizabeth Seton: An American Woman* (New York: America Press, 1938)

Francis and Clare. Translated by Regis J. Armstrong, O.F.M. Cap. and Ignatius C. Brady, O.F.M. (New Jersey: Paulist Press, 1982)

Gies, Francis. *Joan of Arc: The Legend and the Reality* (New York: Harper & Row, 1981)

Goerres, Ida. *The Hidden Face: A Study of St. Thérèse of Lisieux*. Translated by Richard and Clara Winston (New York: Pantheon, 1959)

John of the Cross. *The Collected Works of St. John of the Cross*. (Washington, D.C.: ICS Publications, 1979)

Kazantzakis, Nikos. *Saint Francis*. Translated by P.A. Bien (New York: Simon & Schuster, 1962)

Keyes, F.P. *The Sublime Shepherdess: the Life of Bernadette of Lourdes*. (New York: J. Messner, 1940)

Merton, Thomas. *The Thomas Merton Reader* (New York: New Directions)

Norquist, Marilyn. *How to Read and Pray St. Paul.* (Liguori, MO: Liguori Publications, 1979)

Raymond of Capua. *The Life of Catherine of Siena.* Translated by Conleth Kearns, O.P. (Wilmington, DE: Michael Glazier, 1980)

Teresa of Avila. *The Complete Works.* Edited by Allison Peers (London: Sheed and Ward, 1946) and *The Collected Works of St. Teresa of Avila.* Edited by Kieran Kavanaugh, O.C.D. and Otilio Rodriguez, O.C.D. (Washington, D.C.: ICS Publications, 1980)

Thérèse of Lisieux. *The Story of a Soul.* Translated by John Clarke (Washington, D.C.: ICS Publications, 1976)

Wurmbrand, Richard. *In God's Underground* (Greenwich, CT: Fawcett, 1968)